Samuel Foote

Dramatic Works

Vol. II

Samuel Foote

Dramatic Works
Vol. II

ISBN/EAN: 9783744710114

Printed in Europe, USA, Canada, Australia, Japan

Cover: Foto ©Thomas Meinert / pixelio.de

More available books at **www.hansebooks.com**

THE

DRAMATIC WORKS

OF

SAMUEL FOOTE, Esq;

To which is prefixed

A LIFE OF THE AUTHOR.

In FOUR VOLUMES.

VOL. II.

CONTAINING

The ORATORS.	The LYAR.
The MINOR.	AND The PATRON.

LONDON:

Printed for J. F. and C. RIVINGTON, R. BALDWIN, T. CADELL, W. LOWNDES and S. BLADON. 1788.

THE
ORATORS.

ACT I.

Enter Will Tirehack, *and* Harry Scamper, *booted, with Whips in their Hands, into a Side-Box.*

Scamper.

PSHAW! zounds! prithee, Will, let us go; what signifies our staying here?

Tirehack. Nay, but tarry a little; besides, you know we promised to give Poll Baylifs and Bett Skinner the meeting.

Scamper. No matter, we shall be sure to find them at three at the Shakspeare.

Tirehack. But as we are here, Harry, let us know a little what it's about?

Scamper. About! Why lectures, you fool! Have not you read the bills? and we have plenty of them at Oxford you know!

Tirehack. Well, but for all that, there may be fun.

Scamper. Why then, stay and enjoy it yourself; and I'll step to the Bull and Gate, and call upon Jerry Lack-Latin, and my horse. We shall see you at three. [*Rising.*

Tireback. Nay, but prithee, ſtay.
Scamper. Rot me if I do.
[*Going out of the Box.*
Tireback. Halloo, Harry! Harry—
Scamper. Well, what's the matter now?
[*Returning.*
Tireback. Here's Poll Baylifs come into the gallery.
Scamper. No——
Tireback. She is, by—
Scamper. [*looking.*] Yes, faith! it is ſhe, ſure enough.—How goes it, Poll?
Tireback. Well, now, we ſhall have you, I hope?
Scamper. Ay, if I thought we ſhould get any fun.
Tireback. I'll make an enquiry. Halloo! ſnuffers, ſnuffers!

Enter Candle-ſnuffer.

Your pleaſure, Sir?
Tireback. What is all this buſineſs about here?
Snuffer. Can't ſay, Sir.
Scamper. Well but you could if you would, let us into the ſecret.
Snuffer. Not I, upon my honour!
Tireback. Your honour, you ſon of a whore! D'ye hear, bid your maſter come hither, we want to aſk him a queſtion.
Snuffer. I will— [*Exit.*
Tireback.

Tireback. Scamper, will you aſk him, or ſhall I?

Scamper. Let me alone to him—

Enter FOOTE.

Tireback. O! here he is—

Foote. Your commands with me, gentlemen?

Scamper. Why, you muſt know Will and I here are upon a ſcheme from Oxford; and becauſe caſh begins to run low—How much have you, Will?

Tireback. Three and twenty ſhillings, beſides the crown I paid at the door.

Scamper. And I eighteen; now, as this will laſt us but to-night, we are willing to huſband our time; let us ſee, Will, how are we engaged?

Tireback. Why at three, with Bett and Poll, there, at the Shakſpeare; after that to the Coronation; for you know we have ſeen it but nine times—

Scamper. And then back to the Shakſpeare again; where we ſup, and take horſe at the door.

Tireback. So there's no time to be loſt, you ſee; we deſire, therefore, to know what ſort of a thing this affair here of yours is? What, is it damn'd funny and comical?

Foote. Have you not ſeen the Bills?

Scamper. What, about the lectures? ay, but that's all ſlang, I ſuppoſe; no, no. No tricks

tricks upon travellers; no, we know better—What, are there any more of you; or do you do it all yourself?

Foote. if I was in want of comedians, you gentlemen, are kind enough to lend me a lift; but upon my word, my Intentions, as the bill will inform you, are ferious——

Tireback. Are they? then I'll have my money again. What, do you think we come to London to learn any thing?—Come, Will. [*Going.*

Foote. Hold, Gentleman, I would detain you if poffible. What is it you expect?

Scamper. To be jolly, and laugh, to be fure—

Foote. At what?

Tireback. At what——damme, I don't know—at you, and your frolicks and fancies—

Foote. If that is all you defire, why, perhaps we fhan't difappoint you—

Scamper. Shan't you?—why, that is an honeft fellow—come, begin—

Foote. But you'll be fo kind as not to interrupt me?

Scamper. Never fear——

Foote. Ladies and gentlemen—

[Suds *from the oppofite box calls to* Foote, *and ftops him fhort.*

Suds. Stop a minute; may I be permitted to fpeak?

Foote. Doubtlefs, Sir—

Suds.

Suds. why the affair is this: My wife Alice—for you muſt know my name is Ephraim Suds, I am a ſoap-boiler in the city,—took it into her head, and nothing would ſerve her turn, but that I muſt be a common-council man this year; for, ſays Alice, *ſays ſhe*, It is the *onlieſt* way to riſe in the world.

Foote. A juſt obſervation—you ſucceeded?

Suds. Oh! there was no danger of that—yes, yes, I got it all hollow; but now to come to the marrow of the buſineſs. Well, Alice, ſays I, now I am choſen, what's next to be done? " Why now, ſays Alice, " *ſays ſhe*, thee muſt learn to make ſpeeches; " why doſt not ſee what purferment neigh-" bour Grogram has got; why man, 'tis " all brought about by his *ſpeechifying.* I " tell thee what, Ephraim, if thee can'ſt " but once learn to lay down the law, " there's no knowing to what thee may'ſt " riſe.——"

Foote. Your lady had reaſon.

Suds. Why I thought ſo too; and, as good luck would have it, who ſhould come into the city, in the very nick of time, but maſter profeſſor along with his lectures—Adod, away, in a hurry, Alice and I danced to Pewterers-Hall.

Foote. You improved, I hope?

Suds. O Lud! it is unknown what knowledge we got; we can·read—Oh! we never

never stop to spell a word now—and then he told us such things about verbs, and nouns, and adverbs, that never entered our heads before, and emphasis, and accent; heaven bless us, I did not think there had been such things in the world.

Foote. And have you *speechified* yet?

Suds. Soft; soft and fair; we must walk before we can run—I think I have laid a pretty foundation. The Mansion-house was not built in a day, Master Foote. But to go on with my tale, my dame one day looking over the papers, came running to me; Now, Ephraim, says she, thy business is done; rare news, lad; here is a man at the other end of the town, that will make thee a *speecher* at once, and out she pull'd your proposals. Ah, Alice, says I, thee be'st but a fool, why I know that man, he is all upon his fun; he lecture—why, 'tis all but a bam—Well, 'tis but seeing, says she, so, *wolens nolens*, she would have me come hither; now if so be you be serious, I shall think my money wisely bestowed; but if it be only your comical works, I can tell you, you shall see me no more.

Foote. Sir, I should be extremely sorry to lose you; if I knew but what would content you?

Suds. Why, I want to be made an orator on; and to speak speeches, as I tell you, at

our

our meetings, about politicks, and peace, and addresses, and the new bridge, and all *them* kind of things.

Foote. Why, with your happy talents I should think much might be done.

Suds. I am proud to hear you say so. Indeed I am. I did *speechify* once at a vestry concerning new lettering the church buckets, and came off cutely enough; and, to say the truth, that was the thing that provoked me to go to Pewterers-Hall.

[*Sits down again.*

Foote. Well, Sir, I flatter myself, that in proportion to the difference of abilities in your two instructors, you will here make a tolerable progress. But now, Sir, with your favour, we will proceed to explain the nature of our design, and I hope, in the process, you, gentlemen, will find entertainment, and you, Sir, information.

Mr. FOOTE *then proceeded in his lecture.*

My plan, gentlemen, is to be considered as a superstructure on that admirable foundation laid by the modern professor of English, both our labours tending to the same general end; the perfectioning of our countrymen in a most essential article, the right use of their native language.

But what he has happily begun, I have the vanity to think I have as happily finished; he has, it is true, introduced you into the body of
the

the church, but I conduct you into the choir of the cathedral: Or, to explain myfelf by a more familiar allufion, though he is the Poitier who teaches you the ftep and the grounds; yet I am the Gallini who gives you the air, and the grace of the minuet.

His aim is propriety alone; mine propriety with elegance.

For though reading, fo fhamefully neglected, not only by thofe of tender years, but the adult; not only by children, but even by grown men and women; not only in our private feminaries, but in our public univerfities; is allowed to be a neceffary ingredient towards the formation of an orator; yet, a great many other rules, a great many other precepts are requifite to obtain this perfection.

Nay, perhaps we might, to fupport an argument without the danger of a defeat, at leaft if we may truft obfervation, that of all the profeffions that require a verbal intercourfe with the public, there is no one to which reading is of fo little utility as that of oratory.

I need not infift upon this head, as I believe every gentlemen's experience will furnifh him with inftances of men eminent in oratory, who, from an early vivacity have neglected, or the indulgence of their parents have been emancipated from the attention and application neceffary, it is true, to acquire this rugged art, but at the fame time fo ill-fuited to their tender years, and fo oppofite to
thofe

those innocent amusements in which children are known universally to delight. *Thwart not a child, for you spoil his temper*—is, or at least ought to be, an English proverb, as it is an universal practice.

I would not here be understood to depreciate the usefulness of reading, or to detract from the exceeding merit of the professor's plan; no, my meaning is only just to drop a hint that I may occasionally use him as a walking stick; a kind of an *elegantly clouded Mocoa*, or an *airy Anamaboo*: yet, that it is by no means my intention to depend upon him as a *support*, or lean upon him as a *crutch*; in a word, he will be rather ornamental than necessary to me.

But useless as is his plan to me, I sincerely wish it success for the sake of the public; and if my influence was equal to my inclination, I would have a law enacted, upon the plan of the militia bill, that annually, or biennially, draughts should be made from every parish of two, three, or more, as in that act of able-bodied, so in this of intelligent persons, who at the expence of the several counties, should be sent to the capital, and there compelled to go through as many courses of the professor's lectures as he shall deem sufficient: thus, by those periodical rural detachments, the whole nation will, in a few years, be completely served, and a stock of learning laid in, that will last till time shall be no more.

Would

Would our rulers but adopt this fcheme!
how fuperior would England be even to the
moft illuftrious periods of Greece and Rome!
what an unrivalled happinefs for us, what an
eternal fund of fame for them! Ye Solons, ye
Lycurgus's, ye Numa's, hide your diminifhed
heads; fee what a revolution two laws in a few
years have produced; fee a whole people, funk
in more than Gothic ignorance, accuftomed
to no other iron implements than the pacific
plough-fhare, or the harmlefs fpade, ftart out
at once profound fcholars and veteran foldiers:
If at this happy period, a Frenchman, thinking any thing out of his own country worthy
his attention, fhould condefcend to pay this
kingdom a vifit, methinks, I anticipate the
account he will give of us at his return, (like
his coutryman of old, who, at the taking of
Rome, burfting into the capitol, and there
finding the fenate fixed and immovable in
their feats, declared them an affembly of
kings,) fo will he at once pronounce the
whole Britifh nation to be an army of gene-
rals, and one congregation of doctors. Happy
country! where the *Arma & Toga* are fo for-
tunately blended, as to prevent all contention
for the pre-eminence.

I know but one objection that can be made
to this plan, and that merely a temporary
one; that the culture of our lands will fuftain
an infinite injury, if fuch a number of pea-
fants were to deparochiate, there being already

fcarce

scarce hands sufficient, from the recruits constantly made for Germany, &c. &c. &c. to carry on the common business of husbandry.

But what are riches, perishable commodities, glittering, transitory, fallacious goods, when compared to the substantial, incorruptible endowments of the mind! this truth is indeed, happily inculcated by an old English adage ;

" When lands and goods are gone and spent,
" Then learning is most excellent."

This sensible and poetical distich, I would recommend to Mr. Professor, as a motto for his intended treatise; but I suppose he is already well provided with an apt *Latin*, if not a *Greek* one, to either of which I must yield the preference.

But to wave this ethical argument; I think I can easily foil the force of this objection, by a natural and obvious *Succedaneum*. Suppose a clause was to be added to the bill for the importation of tallow, raw hides, and live cattle from Ireland, that, during this literary emigration, a sufficient number of inhabitants of that country may be transported hither to supply the vacancy : but here it must be observed, that for this purpose an act of parliament is indispensibly necessary; for though it would be difficult, if not impossible, for us, in our present condition, to get in even our harvests, without the aid of hands annually exported

for

for that purpofe from Ireland; yet this is at beft but an illicit trade, and the men themfelves are to be confidered under the article of fmuggled goods: a very heavy penalty being laid by ftatute on all mafters of veffels, who fhall venture to import any of the abovecited commodity into this realm, without fpecial licence; to this purpofe I recollect a cafe in point, the fifth of William and Mary, Ban. Reg. The King contra Oflaarty. Vide V. Rep. vol. iii. chap. 9. page 4.

But if this fhould be thought by the people in power too great an indulgence to the Irifh, as we have never been remarkably profufe in our favours to our loyal and affectionate fifter, I fee no other method of redreffing the imaginary evil, than by exempting from this fervice all the males till a general peace, and accepting, in their room, a fuitable number of difcreet middle-aged females; and thefe when they have been properly perfected in the myfteries of our language, may be returned to their feveral parifhes, and there form little infantine communities of literati, which will be a ftock for the fucceeding generation; and, indeed, upon confideration, I don't know whether this won't prove the beft method for the introduction and univerfal propagation of the plan.

For the Englifh common people, naturally fullen and obftinate, and religioufly attached to their old cuftoms, might be fhocked and
fcan-

scandalized to see, at one bold stroke, the
sescues and sasces, which have been, from
time immemorial, consigned to one, or more
matron in every village, ravished at once from
their hands, and delivered over to the ad-
ministration of the opposite sex.

But to return to my own subject, from
which my zeal for Mr. Professor's success
has tempted me to make rather too long a
digression.

When I ventured to affirm that the profession of an Orator might exist independently
of an accurate knowledge of the arrangement,
and different combinations of the four-and-
twenty letters, so far as (*in the words of the
Professor*) they relate to their being the arbi-
trary marks of meaning upon paper; yet, I
would not be understood to assert this generally, as to every species of oratory, but to
confine myself to those particular branches
only, where the orator's own mind suggests
the matter that his own mouth discharges:
For instance, now, as when affairs of state
are weighed at a common-council, religious
points militated at the Robin-Hood, the arts
and sciences handled in the Strand, or politicks
debated near Westminster-abbey; here the
arguments and words given are supposed to
arise from the immediate impulse of the
giver; but where they are concurrent agents,
as in the oratory peculiar to the pulpit and
the stage, where one individual furnishes

the

the matter, and another adminifters the manner, the cafe is widely different.

In the firft inftance, a tolerable proficiency in reading is indifpenfibly requifite, as fcarce any memory but the late Mr. Heydegger's could retain, to any degree of certainty, the various parts of the Liturgy, the Old and New Teftament, briefs, faculties, excommunications, &c. &c. &c. and a lapfe on thofe folemn occafions might be attended with very aukward circumftances; nor would I here be fuppofed to infinuate, that the pieces of oratory delivered from the pulpit are not the compofition of the deliverer; no—This is fo far from being generally the cafe, that I have often heard complaints made againft particular agents, that they have forced upon their congregations their own crude and infipid productions, when, at the fame time, their native language would furnifh them with fo extenfive and noble a collection of admirable materials. But here the auditor, unlefs he be well read in theology, may be led into a miftake; for there are fome men, who, by a particular happinefs in their manner, have the addrefs to make the works of other men fo abfolutely their own, that there is no diftinguifhing the difference; at this the poet hints in his *male dum recitas*, &c. For thefe various reafons, I think a warm application to the art of reading cannot be too ftrongly

recom-

recommended to the profeſſors of this kind of oratory.

With regard to the profeſſors of the ſtage, tho' reading is undoubtedly uſeful, yet, as the performer is to repeat, and not to read, the deficiency may be ſupplied by the introduction of a third agent, viz. a perſon to read to him till the words are rooted in his memory. This expedient, tho' tedious, I have known frequently practiſed with good ſucceſs: little blunders will now and then unavoidably ariſe, either from the miſapprehenſion of the ſecond agent, or the ignorance or waggery of the third; but theſe ſlips are generally unobſerved, or, thro' inattention or indulgence, overlooked by an audience. But to return to the conſideration of my own plan, from which no temptation ſhall, for the future ſeduce me to digreſs.

We will firſt, then, conſider the utility of oratory.

Secondly, the diſtinct and various kinds, or ſpecies, of that ſcience, as they are practiſed at this day in this kingdom.

Thirdly, we will demonſtrate, that every branch of Engliſh oratory is peculiarly our own, owes its riſe, progreſs, and perfection to this country, and was not only unknown to the ancients, but is intirely repugnant to all thoſe principles they have endeavoured to eſtabliſh.

B   Fourthly,

Fourthly, that any rhetorical fyftem now exifting, inftead of a crofs in the hands, with letters to direct you on your road, will prove only but a Will in the Wifp, to confound, perplex and bewilder you.

Fifthly, from hence will refult a neceffity for the immediate eftablifhment of an academy, for the promulgation and inculcation of modern oratory.

To which academy, the author of thefe propofals does hope, fixthly, that he fhall be appointed perpetual profeffor.

Perhaps it may not be impertinent here to obferve, that the author has induftrioufly avoided, and will, in the courfe of this treatife, avoid all poetical allufion, all grandeur of expreffion, all fplendor of diction; in fhort, renounce every rhetorical prop, as knowing that, on didactic fubjects, order, fimplicity, and perfpicuity, are the means to gain his end, which is not to gratify the imagination, but to improve and polifh the underftanding of my countrymen.

Firft, then, we are to demonftrate the utility of oratory: and, this, we flatter ourfelves, will, in a great meafure, be evident from the confideration of its univerfality, and the diftinctions it procures, both lucrative and honourable, to any man eminent in the art.

There is, by the conftitution of this kingdom, an affembly of many individuals, who, as the feventh fon of a feventh fon is born a
phyfician,

phyfician, are orators by hereditary right;
that is, by birth they are enabled to give their
opinions and fentiments on all fubjects, where
the intereft of their country is concerned: To
this we are to add another affembly, confift-
ing of 558 individuals, where, tho' the fame
privilege is enjoyed as in the firft inftance, yet
this advantage is not poffeffed in virtue of any
inherent natural right, but is obtained in
confequence of an annual, triennial, or fep-
tennial deputation from the whole body of
the people; if then we add to this lift the
number of all thofe candidates who are ambitious of this honour, with the infinite
variety of changes that a revolution of twenty
years will produce, we cannot eftimate thofe
funds of national orators in *effe*, *poffe*, and
velle, to a fmaller quantity than 20,000; and
this, I believe, by the difciples of Demoivre,
will be thought a very moderate computation.

The two orders of the long robe next demand our attention; and as the pre-eminence
is unqueftionably due to the preifthood, let
us confider what number of perfons is neceffary to fupply that fervice? England is divided
into nine thoufand nine hundred and thirteen
parifhes: now, if we fuppofe two paftors for
every parifh, this learned body will be found
to confift of nineteen thoufand eight hundred
and twenty-fix individuals; but as the moft
facred characters are no more exempted from
that fatal ftroke that puts a temporary period

Fourthly, that any rhetorical fyftem now exifting, inftead of a crofs in the hands, with letters to direct you on your road, will prove only but a Will in the Wifp, to confound, perplex and bewilder you.

Fifthly, from hence will refult a neceffity for the immediate eftablifhment of an academy, for the promulgation and inculcation of modern oratory.

To which academy, the author of thefe propofals does hope, fixthly, that he fhall be appointed perpetual profeffor.

Perhaps it may not be impertinent here to obferve, that the author has induftrioufly avoided, and will, in the courfe of this treatife, avoid all poetical allufion, all grandeur of expreffion, all fplendor of diction; in fhort, renounce every rhetorical prop, as knowing that, on didactic fubjects, order, fimplicity, and perfpicuity, are the means to gain his end, which is not to gratify the imagination, but to improve and polifh the underftanding of my countrymen.

Firft, then, we are to demonftrate the utility of oratory: and, this, we flatter ourfelves, will, in a great meafure, be evident from the confideration of its univerfality, and the diftinctions it procures, both lucrative and honourable, to any man eminent in the art.

There is, by the conftitution of this kingdom, an affembly of many individuals, who, as the feventh fon of a feventh fon is born a

phyfician,

THE ORATORS. 19

phyſician, are orators by hereditary right; that is, by birth they are enabled to give their opinions and ſentiments on all ſubjects, where the intereſt of their country is concerned: To this we are to add another aſſembly, conſiſting of 558 individuals, where, tho' the ſame privilege is enjoyed as in the firſt inſtance, yet this advantage is not poſſeſſed in virtue of any inherent natural right, but is obtained in conſequence of an annual, triennial, or ſeptennial deputation from the whole body of the people; if then we add to this liſt the number of all thoſe candidates who are ambitious of this honour, with the infinite variety of changes that a revolution of twenty years will produce, we cannot eſtimate thoſe funds of national orators in *eſſe*, *poſſe*, and *velle*, to a ſmaller quantity than 20,000; and this, I believe, by the diſciples of Demoivre, will be thought a very moderate computation.

The two orders of the long robe next demand our attention; and as the pre-eminence is unqueſtionably due to the preiſthood, let us conſider what number of perſons is neceſſary to ſupply that ſervice? England is divided into nine thouſand nine hundred and thirteen pariſhes: now, if we ſuppoſe two paſtors for every pariſh, this learned body will be found to conſiſt of nineteen thouſand eight hundred and twenty-ſix individuals; but as the moſt ſacred characters are no more exempted from that fatal ſtroke that puts a temporary period grounded our calculation on the number of parishes, we shall in this derive our computation from the number of houses in the kingdom.

To any man tolerably acquainted with the country of England, it is unneceffary to observe, that not only in every town, but almoſt in every hamlet through which he travels, his eyes are conſtantly caught by the appearance of a ſmart houſe, prefaced with white rails, and prologued by a red door, with a braſs knocker; when you deſire to be acquainted with the name and quality of the owner of this manſion, you are always told that it belongs to lawyer ſuch a one: now, if a hamlet containing thirty houſes, with perhaps an environ of an equal number, where labour and the fruits of the earth are the only ſources of wealth, can ſupport one attorney in this rural magnificence, what an infinite number of lawyers can a commerical capital ſuſtain? But becauſe I would rather retrench than exceed, I will only quarter one attorney upon fifty houſes. The number of houſes in the reign of George the Firſt (ſince which time the quantity is conſiderably encreaſed,) was computed at 1,175,951. The number of attorneys then will be 23,518; and, if we reckon one barriſter to twenty attorneys, the ſum total is 24,693.

I know it will be here objected, that but one ſmall part of this numerous body can be
benefited

benefited by my plan, the privilege of speaking publickly being permitted to the superior order, the barristers alone: but this criticism is confined to the observation of what passes merely in Westminster-Hall, without considering that, at every quarter and petty session at all county-courts, courts-leet, courts-baron, &c. &c. &c. full power of pleading is permitted to every practitioner of the law.

As the number of those who incorporate themselves to promote, not only with their cash but their counsel, the progress of the arts and sciences, is unlimitted, it will be impossible for any fixed period to ascertain their quantity: nor can we, with any certainty, as the Court-Register has been silent to the members of common-council, determine the amount of the city orators; besides, as what has been already offered is more than sufficient to prove the utility of our scheme from its universality, we shall not trouble our readers nor ourselves with any further calculations; for tho' they are replete with great depth of knowledge, are the result of intense application, and the vehicles of mathematical truths, yet to the million the disquisition is but dry and tedious, and our purpose always was, and is, to mix with our instruction a proper portion of delection.

We will, therefore, for these reasons, hasten to the consideration of the second point proposed, propofed, viz. An inquiry into the various kinds of oratory now exifting in this country. And we fhall not, on this occafion, trouble ourfelves with the invefligation of all the fmaller branches of this art; but, like the profeffors in anatomy, contenting ourfelves with the diffection of the noble parts, remit the examination of the ignoble ones to the care of fubaltern artifts. Leaving, then, to the minute Philofophers of the age all the orators of veftries, clubs, and coffee-houfes, *Paulo majora canamus*; and for the better illuftration of this head, permit me, reader, to be a little fanciful. We will fuppofe oratory to be one large tree, of which tree fcience is the *radix*; eloquence the trunk; from which trunk fprout nine diftinct ramifications; from which ramifications depends a fruit peculiar to each. But to make this clearer, we will prefent thee with the tree itfelf, not enigmatically hieroglyfied, but plainly and palpably pourtrayed,

Archbifhops

THE ORATORS.

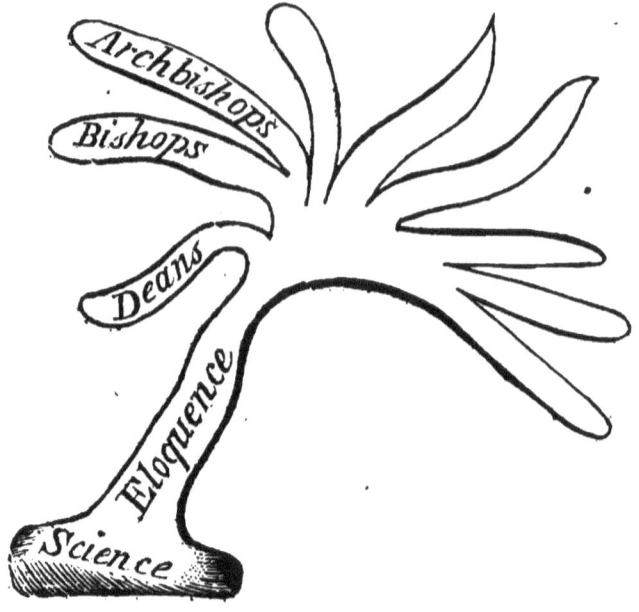

But here, reader, let me not arrogate to myſelf the merit of this happy explication; I own the hint was firſt given me with my Grammar. The ingenious, profound Lilly, after he has led his pupils through the various, and almoſt impervious provinces of nouns, pronouns, verbs, participles, and adverbs, conducts them to the foot of that arduous and ſtupendous mountain *Qui Mihi*: here, dreading leſt their youthful ardour might be damp'd with the ſteep aſcent, he reanimates their ſlackened nerves with the myſtic picture of an apple-tree, the acceſs to whoſe boughs, though tedious and difficult, will yet

yet be amply rewarded by leave to revel uncontrouled through the whole region of pepins. May the luscious fruit sprouting from the apex of each of my ramifications prove an equal spur to every beardless orator!

I don't know whether the mentioning another order of orators, as they are not at present existing in this kingdom, may not be deemed an impropriety. But as I am a sincere lover of my country, I can't help recommending an immediate importation of some of those useful and able artists. Sir William Temple, in his Essay on Poetry, has recorded their virtues; and as the race was not extinguished in his time, it is to be hoped that it still remains.

In Ireland, says Sir William, the great men of their septs, among many officers of their family, had not only a physician, a huntsman, a smith, and such like, but a poet and tale-teller.

The first recorded and sung the actions of their ancestors, and entertained the company at feasts; the latter amused them with tales, when they were melancholy and could not sleep: and a very gallant gentleman has told me, of his own experience, that in his wolf-hunting there, when he used to be abroad in the mountains three or four days together, and lye very ill at nights, so as he could not well sleep, they would bring one of those tale-tellers, that when he lay down would
begin

begin a ftory of a king, or a giant, a dwarf
and a damfel, and continue all night long in
fuch an even tone that you heard him going
on whenever you awakened; and he believed
nothing any phyficians could give had fo
good and fo innocent an effect to make men
fleep in any pains or diftempers of body or
mind. Thefe are Sir William Temple's words,
which contain an amazing inftance of the
power of thofe orators over the paffions, it
requiring full as much art and addrefs to af-
fuage and quell, as to blow up, and excite,
a tumult in the mind.

In a bill not long fince depending in parliament, for the better regulating the city-
watch, a claufe was recommended, by a late
refpectable magiftrate, that, to prevent the
watchmen from fleeping at nights on bulks
(the fource of many diforders) the faid watchmen fhould be compelled to fleep fix hours in
the day; an arch member feconded the motion, and begged to be included in this claufe;
for that being grievoufly afflicted with the
gout, he could not for many days fleep a fingle
wink; now if he could be compelled to take
a fix hours fleep every day, he apprehended
that his fits would be of a much fhorter du-
ration. Upon this dry comment, the motion was rafhly rejected; but if the houfe had
received the leaft intimation of the aftonifh-
ing abilities of the Rockers, (for by that appellation I choofe to diftinguifh this order of
orators,)

orators,) I am convinced that the above clauſe would not only have been received, but that proper encouragement would have been given, by parliament, for the introduction and eſtabliſhment of this uſeful oratorical ſect.

Nor, indeed conſidering the vaſt addition to our cuſtomary cares, from the unaccountable fluctuation of our funds, the cauſe of concern to many thouſand individuals, do I think a viſit from a convenient quantity of thoſe artiſts would be now out of ſeaſon; but how this honour is to be obtained, whether any of theſe great men are now reſiding amongſt us, under the diſguiſe of chairmen and hackney coachmen; or whether it would not be more adviſeable to employ thoſe gentlemen who have ſo lately and ſuccefsfully rummaged the Highlands of Scotland and Ireland for the remains of Runic poetry in ſearch of the ableſt profeſſors; is ſubmitted to the Society for the Encouragement of Arts.

I am aware that, on this occaſion, ſome arch wag, poſſeſſed of the ſame ſpirit with the above ſenator, will object to my ſcheme of importation, by alledging, that we have of our own growth an ample proviſion of rockers, and refer us for proof to our ſeveral churches and chapels, during the hours of eleven and two on a Sunday, where the ſleep-compelling power will be experimentally demonſtrated to exiſt in its full force amongſt us; but not to derogate from the abilities of my countrymen,

men, surely the shortness of the time, the cause of the nap, rarely continuing above fifteen or sixteen minutes, will not admit of a proper experiment: besides, how can one orator supply a whole parish, unless, indeed our churches were to be converted into dormitories, which I can't think will happen, as this would be attended with inconveniencies too obvious to need a recital.

Abstracted from this last order, the English orators are to be divided into four distinct classes, the pulpit, the senate, the bar, and the stage; with the first of these branches, the pulpit, I shan't interfere, and, indeed, so few people now of consequence and consideration frequent the churches, that the art is scarce worth cultivation. The bar—

Scamper. Pshaw! there's enough of this dull prosing; come, give us a little of something that's funny; you talked about pupils. Could not we see them?

Foote. Rather too precipitate, Sir; but however, in some measure to satisfy you, and demonstrate the success of our scheme; give me leave to introduce to you a most extraordinary instance, in the person of a young Highlander. It is not altogether a year since this astonishing subject spoke nothing but Erse. Encouraged by the prodigies of my brother professor's skill, whose fame, like the Chevalier Taylor's, pierces the remotest regions, his relations were tempted to send this young genius to Edinburgh; where he
went

went through a regular courfe of the profeffor's lectures, to finifh his ftudies; he has been about fix weeks under my care, and, confidering the time, I think you will be amazed at his progrefs. Donald !—

Enter Donald.

What's yer wull, Sir?
Foote. Will you give thefe ladies and gentlemen a proof of your fkill?
Donald. Ah, ye wad ha' a fpecimen of my oratorical art.
Foote. If you pleafe.
Donald. In gude troth on ye fal; wol ye gi' me a topick?
Foote. O! chufe for yourfelf.
Donald. Its aw one to Donald.
Foote. What think you of a fhort panegyrick on the fcience we are treating of?
Donald. On oratory? wi' aw my heart.
Foote. Mind your action; let that accompany your words—
Donald. Dunna heed, mon—The topick I prefum to haundle, is the miraculous gifts of an orator, wha' by the bare power of his words, he leads men, women, and bairns as he lifts—
Scamper. And who?
Donald. [*tartly.*] Men, women, and bairns.
Scamper. Bairns; who are they?

Foote.

Foote. Oh! children——his meaning is obvious enough.

Donald. Ay, ay; men, women, and bairns, wherever he lifts; and firſt for the antiquity of the art—Ken ye, my lads, wha was the firſt orator?—Mayhap, ye think it was Tully, the Latineſt; ye are wide o'the mark; or Demoſthenes the Greek? In gude troth, ye're as far off as before—Wha was it then? It was e'en that arch-chiel, the Deevil himſel—

Scamper. [*Haſtily.*] The devil it was; how do you prove that?

Donald. Guds zounds, mon, ye brake the thrid of my harang; an ye'll but ha'd yer tongue, I'ſe prove it as plain as a pike-ſtaff.

Tireback. Be quiet, Will, and let him go on.

Donald. I ſay it was that arch-chiel, the Deevil himſel. Ye ken weel, my lads, how Adam and Eve were planted in Eden, wi' plenty o' bannocks and cail, and aw that they wiſhed, but were prohibited the eating of pepins——

Scamper. Apples——

Donald. Weel, weel, and are na pepins and apples aw the ſame thing?

Foote. Nay, pray, Gentlemen, hear him out. Go on with your pepins——

Donald. Prohibited the eating of pepins; upon which what does me the orator Satan, but he whiſpers a ſaft ſpeech in her lug; egad

egad our grannum fell to in an inftant, and eat a pepin without ftaying to pare it— (*Addreffes himfelf to the Oxonians.*) Ken ye lads, wha was the firft orator, now?

Tireback. [*to Scamper.*] What fay you to that?

Scamper. By my foul, the fellow's right—

Donald. Ay, but ye wan'na ha' patience— ye wan'na ha' patience, lads—

Tireback. Hold your jaw, and go on—

Donald. Now, we come to the definition of an orator; and it is from the Latin words *oro, orare,* to intreat, or perfwad; and how, by the means o' elocution, or argument, which argument confifts o' letters, which letters, joined mak fyllables, which fyllables compounded mak words, which words combined mak fentences, or periods, or which aw together mak an orator, fo the firft gift of an orator is words—

Scamper. Here, Donald, you are out.

Donald. How fo?

Scamper. Words, the firft gift of an orator! No, Donald, no, at fchool I learned better than that: Do'ft not remember, Will, what is the firft perfection of an orator? action. The fecond, action. The third, action.

Tireback. Right, right, Harry, as right as my nail; there, Donald, I think he has given you a dofe—

Donald. An ye ftay me, i' the midft o' my argument—

Scamper.

THE ORATORS. 33

Scamper. Why don't you ſtick to truth?
Donald. I tell ye, I can *logically.*
Tireback. Damn your logick——
Donald. Mighty weel—Maiſter Foote, how ca' ye this uſage?
Foote. Oh! never mind them——proceed.
Donald. In gude troth, I'ſe nat ſay ane word mare.
Foote. Finiſh, finiſh, Donald.——
Donald. Ah! they have jumbled aw my ideas together; but an they will enter into a fair argumentation, I'ſe convince 'em that Donald Macgregor is mare than a match.——
Scamper. You be——
Donald. Very weel——
Foote. Nay, but my dear Donald——
Donald. Hands aff, Maiſter Foote——I ha' finiſhed my tale, the De'el a word mare ſal ye get out o' Donald——yer ſervant, Sir.
[*Exit.*
Foote. You ſee, gentlemen, what your impatience has loſt us.
Scamper. Rot him, let him go; but is this fellow one of your *pupils?* why, what a damnable twang he has got, with his men, women, and bairns!——
Foote. His pronunciation is, I own, a little irregular; but then conſider he is but merely a novice; why, even in his preſent condition, he makes no bad figure for his five minutes at the *Robin-Hood*; and in a month or two,
C we

we shan't be ashamed to start him in a more *respectable place.*

But now, gentlemen, we are to descend to the peculiar essential qualities of each distinct species of oratory; and first for the bar—but as no didactic rules can so well convey, or words make a proper impression, we will have recourse to more palpable means, and endeavour, by a lively imitation, to demonstrate the extent of our art. We must, for this end, employ the aid of our pupils; but as some preparation is necessary, we hope you will indulge us in a short interruption.

End of the First Act.

ACT II.

SCENE, A Hall of Justice.

Enter FOOTE.

THE first species of Oratory we are to demonstrate our skill in, is that of the bar; and, in order to give our lecture an air of reality, you are to suppose this a court of justice, furnished with proper ministers to discharge the necessary functions. But, to supply these gentlemen with business, we must likewise institute an imaginary cause; and, that the whole may be ideal, let it be the prosecution of an imaginary being; I mean the phantom of Cock-lane, a phænomenon that has much puzzled the brains, and terrified the minds, of many of our fellow-subjects.

You are to consider, ladies and gentlemen, that the language of the bar is a species of oratory distinct from every other. It has been observed, that the ornaments of this profession have not shone with equal lustre in an assembly near their own hall; the reason assigned, though a pleasant, is not the true *one*. It has been hinted, that these gentlemen were in want of their briefs; but was that the

the difeafe, the remedy would be eafy enough: they need only have recourfe to the *artifice* fuccefsfully practifed by fome of their colleagues; inftead of having their briefs in their hands, to hide them at the bottom of their hats.

[*Calls to his pupils, who enter dreffed as a juftice, a clerk, a ferjeant at law, and a counfellor.*]

You will remember, gentlemen, your proper paufes, repetitions, hums, ha's, and interjections: now feat yourfelves, and you the counfel remember to be mighty dull, and you the juftice to fall afleep. I muft prepare to appear in this caufe as a witnefs.

[*Exit.*

Juftice. Clerk, read the Indictment.

Clerk *Reads.*

Middlefex, to wit.

Fanny Phantom, you are indicted, That on or before the firft day of January, 1762, you the faid Fanny did, in a certain houfe, in a certain ftreet, called Cock-lane, in the county of Middlefex, malicioufly, treacheroufly, wickedly, and wilfully, by certain thumpings, knockings, fcratchings, and flutterings againft doors, walls, wainfcots, bedfteads, and bedpofts, difturb, annoy, affault, and terrify divers innocent, inoffenfive, harmlefs, quiet, fimple people, refiding in, at, near or about the faid Cock-lane, and elfewhere, in the faid county of Middlefex, to the great prejudice of

THE ORATORS.

of said people in said county. How say you, guilty, or——

Counsellor stops the Clerk short.

May it please your worship—hem—I am counsel in this cause for the ghost—hem—and before I can permit her to plead, I have an objection to make, that is—hem—I shall object to her pleading at all.—Hem—It is the standing law of this country—hem—and has—hem—always been so allowed, deemed, and practised, that—hem—all criminals should be tried *par pares*, by their equals—hem—that is—hem—by a jury of equal rank with themselves. Now, if this be the case, as the case it is; I—hem—I should be glad to know, how my client can be tried in this here manner. And first, who is my client? She is in the indictment called a phantom, a ghost; What is a ghost? a spirit. What is a spirit? a spirit is a thing that exists independently of, and is superior to, flesh and blood. And can any man go for to think, that I can advise my client to submit to be tried by people of an inferior rank to herself? certainly no—I therefore, humbly move to squash this indictment, unless a jury of ghosts be first had, and obtained; unless a jury of ghosts be first had and obtained. [*Sits down.*

Serjeant. I am, in this cause, Counsel against Fanny Phantom the ghost;—eh,—and notwithstanding the rule laid down by Mr.

Mr. Profequi, be—eh—right in the main, yet here it can't avail his client a whit. We allow—eh—we do allow, pleafe your worfhip, that Fanny *quoad* Phantom,—eh—had originally a right to a jury of ghofts; but—eh—if fhe did, by any act of her own, forfeit this right, her plea cannot be admitted. Now, we can prove, pleafe your worfhip, prove by a cloud of witneffes, that faid Fanny did, as fpecified in the indictment, fcratch, knock, and flutter;—eh—which faid fcratchings, knockings, and flutterings—eh—being operations, merely peculiar to flefh, blood, and body—eh—we do humbly apprehend—eh—that by condefcending to execute the aforefaid operations, fhe has waved her privilege as a ghoft, and may be tried in the ordinary form, according to the ftatute fo made and provided in the reign of, &c. &c. &c.

Your worfhip's opinion.

Tireback. Smoke the juftice, he is as faft as a church.

Scamper. I fancy he has touched the tankard too much this morning; he'll know a good deal of what they have been faying.

Juftice. [*Is waked by the Clerk, who tells him they have pleaded.*] Why the objection—oh—brought by Mr. Profequi, is (*whifpers the clerk*) doubtlefs provifionally a valid objection; but then, if the culprit has, by an act of her own, defeated her privilege, as afferted in Mr. Serjeant's replication; we conceive
fhe

she may be legally tried—oh,—besides—oh,
—besides, I, I, I can't well see how we
could impannel a jury of ghosts; or—oh—
how twelve spirits, who have no body at all
can be said to take a corporal oath, as required by law—unless, indeed, as in case of
the peerage, the prisoner may be tried on
their honour.

Counsellor. Your worship's distinction is
just; knockings, scratchings, &c. as asserted
by Mr. Serjeant.——

Serjeant. Asserted—Sir, do you doubt my
instructions?

Counsellor. No interruptions, if you please,
Mr. Serjeant; I say as asserted, but can
assertions be admitted as proofs? certainly
no——

Serjeant. Our evidence is ready——

Counsellor. To that we object, to that we
object, as it will anticipate the merits—your
worship——

Serjeant. Your worship——

Justice. Why, as you impeach the ghost's
privilege, you must produce proofs of her
scratchings.

Serjeant. Call Shadrach Bodkin.

Clerk. Shadrach Bodkin, come into court.

Enter Bodkin.

Serjeant. Pray, Mr. Bodkin, where do you
live?

C 4 *Bodkin.*

Bodkin. I fojourn in Lukener's-lane.
Serjeant. What is your profeffion?
Bodkin. I am a *teacher* of the *word,* and a *taylor.*
Scamper. Zounds, Will, it is a methodift.
Tireback. No, fure!
Scamper. By the lord Harry, it is.
Clerk. Silence.
Serjeant. Do you know any thing of Fanny the Phantom?
Bodkin. Yea—I do.
Serjeant. Can you give any account of her thumpings, fcratchings, and flutterings?
Bodkin. Yea——manifold have been the fcratchings and knockings that I have heard.
Serjeant. Name the times.
Bodkin. I have attended the fpirit *Fanny* from the firft day of her flutterings, even to the laft fcratch fhe gave.
Serjeant. How long may that be?
Bodkin. Five weeks did fhe flutter, and fix weeks did fhe fcratch.
Scamper. Six weeks—Damn it, I wonder fhe did not wear out her nails.
Clerk. Silence.
Serjeant. I hope the court is convinced.
Counfellor. Hold, Mafter Bodkin; you and I muft have a little difcourfe. A taylor, you fay. Do you work at your bufinefs?
Bodkin. No—
Counfellor. Look upon me, look upon the court

court—Then your prefent trade is your teaching?
 Bodkin. It is no trade.
 Counfellor. What is it then, a calling?
 Bodkin. No, it is no calling—it is rather—as I may fay—a *forcing*—a *compelling*—
 Counfellor. By whom?
 Bodkin. By the fpirit that is within me—
 Scamper. It is an evil fpirit, I believe; and needs muft when the devil drives, you know, Will.
 Tireback. Right, Harry—
 Counfellor. When did you firft feel thefe fpiritual motions?
 Bodkin. In the town of Norwich, where I was born;—One day as I was fitting crofs-legged on my fhop-board, new feating a cloth pair of breeches of Mr. Alderman Crape's—I felt the fpirit within me, moving upwards and downwards, and this way and that way, and tumbling and jumbling—at firft I thought it was the colic—
 Counfellor. And how are you certain it was not?
 Bodkin. At laft I heard a voice whifpering within me, crying, Shadrach, Shadrach, Shadrach, caft away the things that belong to thee, thy thimble and fheers, and do the things that I bid thee.
 Counfellor. And you did?
 Bodkin. Yea, verily.

Counfellor.

Counsellor. I think I have heard a little of you, Master Bodkin; and so you quitted your business, your wife, and your children?
Bodkin. I did.
Counsellor. You did—But then you communed with other men's wives?
Bodkin. Yea, and with widows, and with maidens.
Counsellor. How came that about, Shadrach?
Bodkin. I was moved thereunto by the spirit.
Counsellor. I should rather think by the flesh—I have been told, friend Bodkin, that twelve became pregnant——
Bodkin. Thou art deceived—They were barely but nine.
Counsellor. Why, this was an active spirit.
Serjeant. But to the point, Mr. Prosequi.
Counsellor. Well, then—you say you have heard those scratchings and knockings?
Bodkin. Yea——
Counsellor. But why did you think they came from a spirit?
Bodkin. Because the very same thumps, scratches, and knocks, I have felt on my breast-bone from the spirit within me——
Counsellor. And these noises you are sure you heard on the first of January?
Bodkin. Certain——
Serjeant. But to what do all those interrogatories tend?
Counsellor.

THE ORATORS. 43

Counſellor. To a moſt material purpoſe; your worſhip obſerves, that Bodkin is poſitive as to the noiſes made on the firſt day of January by Fanny the Phantom: now if we can prove an *Alibi*, that is, that, on that very day, at that very time, the ſaid Fanny was ſcratching and fluttering any where elſe, we apprehend that we deſtroy the credit of this witneſs—Call Peter Paragraph.

Clerk. Peter Paragraph, come into court.

Counſellor. This gentlemen is an eminent printer, and has collected, for the public information, every particular relative to this remarkable ſtory; but as he has the misfortune to have but one leg, your worſhip will indulge him in the uſe of a chair.

Clerk. Peter Paragraph, come into court.

Enter Paragraph.

Counſellor. Pray, Mr. Paragraph where was you born?

Paragraph. Sir, I am a native of Ireland, and born and bred in the city of Dublin.

Counſellor. When did you arrive in the city of London?

Paragraph. About the laſt autumnal equinox; and now I recollect, my *Journal* makes mention of my departure for England, in the Beſsborough Packet, Friday, October the tenth, N. S. or New Stile.

Counſellor.

Counsellor. Oh! then the Journal is yours?

Paragraph. Pleafe your worfhip, it is; and relating thereto I believe I can give you a pleafant conceit—Laft week I went to vifit a *peer*, for I know *peers*, and *peers* know me. Quoth his lordfhip to me, Mr. Paragraph, with refpect to your Journal, I would wifh that your paper was whiter, or your ink blacker. Quoth I to the peer, by way of *reply*, I hope you will own there is enough for the money; his lordfhip was pleafed to laugh. It was fuch a pretty repartee, he, he, he, he——

Juftice. Pray, Mr. Paragraph, what might be your bufinefs in England?

Paragraph. Hem——a little love affair, pleafe your worfhip.

Counsellor. A wife, I fuppofe——

Paragraph. Something tending that way; even fo long ago as January 1739-40, there paft fome amorous glances between us; fhe is the daughter of old Vamp of the Turnftile; but at that time I ftifled my paffion, Mrs. Paragraph being then in the land of the living.

Counsellor. She is now dead?

Paragraph. Three years and three quarters, pleafe your worfhip: we were exceeding happy together; fhe was, indeed, a little apt to be jealous.

Counsellor. No wonder——

Paragraph.

THE ORATORS.

Paragraph. Yes: they can't help it, poor fouls; but notwithftanding, at her death, I gave her a prodigious good character in my Journal.

Counfellor. And how proceeds the prefent affair?

Paragraph. Juft now, we are quite at a ftand——

Counfellor. How fo?

Paragraph. The old fcoundrel her father has played me a flippery trick.

Counfellor. Indeed!

Paragraph. As he could give no money in hand, I agreed to take her *fortune* in copies; I was to have the Wits *Vade Mucum* entire; four hundred of news from the invifible world, in fheets; all that remained of Glanvil upon Witches; Hill's Bees, Bardana, Brewing, and Balfam of Honey, and three eights of Robinfon Crufoe.

Counfellor. A pretty fortune!

Paragraph. Yes; they are things that ftir in the trade; but you muft know that we agreed to go halves in Fanny the Phantom. But whilft I and two authors, whom I had hired to afk queftions, at nine fhillings a night, were taking notice of the knockings at the houfe of Mr. Parfons himfelf, that old rafcal Vamp had privately printed off a thoufand eighteenpenny fcratchings, purchafed of two methodift preachers, at the public houfe over the way——

Counfellor.

Counsellor. Now we come to the point—look upon this evidence; was he present at Mr. Parsons's knockings?

Paragraph, Never; this is one of the rascally methodists—Harkee, fellow, how could you be such a scoundrel to sell for genuine your counterfeit scratchings to Vamp?

Bodkin. My scratchings were the true scratchings—

Paragraph. Why, you lying son of a whore, did not I buy all my materials from the girl's father himself?

Bodkin. What the spirit commanded, that did I.

Paragraph. What spirit?

Bodkin. The spirit within me—

Paragraph. If I could but get at you, I would soon try what sort of a spirit it is—stop, you villain.—[*Exit* Bodkin.]—The rogue has made his escape—but I will dog him, to find out his haunts, and then return for a warrant—His scratchings! a scoundrel; I will have justice, or I'll turn his tabernacle into a pigstye. [*Exit* Paragraph.

Counsellor. I hope, please your worship, we have sufficiently established our *Alibi.*

Justice. You are unquestionably entitled to a jury of ghosts.

Counsellor. Mr. Serjeant, you will provide us a list?

Serjeant. Let us see—you have no objection
to

to Sir George Villars; the evil genius of Brutus; the ghoſt of Banquo; Mrs. Veal.

Counſellor. We object to a woman—your worſhip—

Juſtice. Why, it is not the practice; this, it muſt be owned, is an extraordinary caſe. But, however, if, on conviction, the Phantom ſhould plead pregnancy, Mrs. Veal will be admitted into the jury of matrons.

Serjeant. I thank your worſhip: then the court is adjourned.

[Terence *and* Dermot *in an upper box.*
Terence. By my ſhoul, but I will ſpake.
Dermot. Arrah, be quiet, Terence.
Terence. Dibble burn me but I will; hut, hut, not ſpake, what ſhould ail me? harkee you, Mr. Juſtice—
Scamper. Halloo, what's the matter now, Will?
Dermot. Leave off, honey Terence, now you are well—
Terence. Dermot, be eaſy—
Scamper. Hear him—
Tireback. Hear him—
Terence. Ay, hear him, hear him; why the matter is this, Mr. Juſtice, that little hopping fellow there, that Dublin Journal man, is as great a liar as ever was born—
Tireback. How ſo?
Terence. Ay, prithee don't bodder me; what, dy'e learn no more manners at Oxford college, than to ſtop a gentleman in the midſt of

of his speech before he begins? oh, for shame of yourself—Why the matter is this, Mr. Justice, that there what the dehble dy'e call him, Pra-Praragraf, but by my shoul, that is none of his name neither, I know the little bastard as well as myself; as to Fanny the Phantom, long life to the poor gentlewoman, he knows no more of her than the mother that bore her——

Suds. Indeed! good lord, you surprise me!

Terence. Arrah, now, honey Suds, spake when you are spoke to; you arn't upon the jury, my jewel, now; by my shoul you are a little too fat for a ghost.

Tireback. Prithee, friend Ephraim, let him go on; let's hear a little what he would be at——

Terence. I say, he knows nothing about the case that is litigated here, d'ye see, at all, at all;· because why, I hant-ha been from Dublin above four weeks, or a month; and I saw him in his shop every day; so how could he be here and there too? unless, indeed, he used to fly backwards and forwards, and that you see is impossible, because why, he has got a wooden leg.

Scamper. What the devil is the fellow about?

Tireback. I smoke him—harkee, Terence, who do you take that lame man to be?

Terence. Oh, my jewel, I know him well enough

enough fure by his parfon, for all he thought to conceal himfelf by changing his name——
Scamper. Why, it is Foote, you fool.
Terence. Arrah, who?
Tireback. Foote.
Terence. Fot, what the lecture-man? Pa—
Tireback. Yes.
Terence. Arrah, be eafy, honey——
Scamper. Nay, enquire of Suds.
Suds. Truly I am minded 'twas he.
Terence. Your humble fervant yourfelf, Mr. Suds; by my fhoul, I'll wager you three thirteens to a rap, that it is no fuch matter at all, at all.
Scamper. Done——and be judged by the company.
Terence. Done—I'll afk the orator himfelf —here he comes;

Enter FOOTE.

harkee, honey Fot, was it yourfelf that was happing about here but now?
Foote. I have heard your debate, and muft give judgment againft you——
Terence. What, yourfelf, yourfelf!
Foote. It was——
Terence. Then, faith, I have loft my thirteens—Arrah, but Fot, my jewel, why are you after playing fuch pranks to bring an honeft jontleman into company where he is

nat——But what is this felling of lectures a thriving profeſſion?

Foote. I can't determine as yet; the public have been very indulgent; I have not long opened.

Terence. By my fhoul, if it anfwers, will you be my pupil and learn me the trade?

Foote. Willingly——

Terence. That's an honeſt fellow, long life to you, lad. [*Sits down.*

Enter M'George.

M'George. Here is Doctor Frifcano without.

Foote. Frifcano—who is he?

M'George. The German phyſician from James-Street.

Foote. Well; what is his bufinefs with me?

M'George. He is in danger of lofing his trade.

Foote. How fo?

M'George. He fays, laſt fummer, things went on glibly enough, for then he had the market all to himſelf; but this year there is an Italian fellow ſtarted up in the garden, that with his face and grimace has taken all his patients away.

Foote. That's hard.

M'George. Dreadful——if you was to hear the poor man's terrible tale you would really be be moved to compaſſion: he ſays that his bleeding won't find him in bread; and as to the tooth trade; excepting two ſtumps, for ſixpence a piece, 'tis a month ſince he looked in a mouth——.

Foote. How can I help him?

M'George. Why he thinks oratory will do all with the Engliſh; and if you would but teach him to talk, he ſhould get his cuſtom again——

Foote. Can he read?

M'George. Oh Lord! poor man, no.

Foote. Well let him attend here on——

M'George. He hopes that you will quickly diſpatch him, for if he finds he can't do as a doctor, he intends to return to the curing of horſes again.

Foote. Well, tell him he may reſt aſſured, he ſhall either bleed or ſhoe in a fortnight.

[*Exit* M'George.

Foote. Having thus completed our lecture on the eloquence peculiar to the bar, we ſhall produce one great group of orators, in which will be exhibited ſpecimens of every branch of the art. You will have, at one view, the choleric, the placid, the voluble, the frigid, the frothy, the turgid, the calm, and the clamorous; and as a proof of our exquiſite ſkill, our ſubjects are not ſuch as a regular education has prepared for the reception of this ſublime ſcience, but a ſet of illiterate mechanics,

chanics, whom you are to suppose assembled at the Robin-Hood in the Butcher-row, in order to discuss and adjust the various systems of Europe; but particularly to determine the separate interest of their own mother country.

End of the Second Act.

ACT III.

SCENE, *The Robin-Hood.*

The PRESIDENT.

Dermot O'Droheda, *a Chairman*; Tim Twift, *a Taylor*; Strap, *a Shoemaker*; Anvil, *a Smith*; Sam Slaughter, *a Butcher*; Catchpole, *a Bailiff.* All with pewter pots before them.

PRESIDENT.

SILENCE, gentlemen; are your pots replenifhed with porter?
All. Full, Mr. Prefident.
Prefident. We will then proceed to the bufinefs of the day; and let me beg, gentlemen, that you will, in your debates, preferve that decency and decorum that is due to the importance of your deliberations, and the dignity of this illuftrious affembly.—[*Gets up, pulls off his hat, and reads the motion.*]—Motion made laft Monday to be debated to-day, " That, for the future, inftead of that vulgar " potation called porter, the honourable
" members

"members may be supplied with a proper
"quantity of Irish usquebagh.
"Dermot O'Droheda + his mark."
O'Droheda. [*Gets up.*] That's I myself.
President. Mr. Q'Droheda.
O'Droheda. Mr. President, the case is this; it is not becase I am any great lover of that same usquebagh that I have set my mark to the motion; but becase I did not think it was decent for a number of gontlemen that were, d'ye see, met to settle the affairs of the nation, to be guzzling a pot of porter; to be sure the liquor is a pretty sort of a liquor enough when a man is hot with trotting between a couple of poles; but this is anotherguess matter, becase why, the head is concerned; and if it was not for the malt and the haps, dibble burn me but I would as soon take a drink from the Thames as your porter. But as to usquebagh; ah, long life to the liquor—it is an exhilirator of the bowels, and a stomatic to the head; I say, Mr. President, it invigorates, it stimulates, it—in short it is the onliest liquor of life, and no man alive will die whilst he drinks it.

[*Sits down. Twist gets up, having a piece of paper, containing the heads of what he says, in his hat.*
President. Mr. Timothy Twist.
Tim Twist. Mr. President, I second Mr. O'Droheda's motion; and, sir, give me leave
—I say,

—I say, Mr. President—[*looks in his hat*]—give me leave to observe, that, sir, tho' it is impossible to add any force to what has been advanced by my honourable friend in the straps; yet, sir,—[*looks in his hat again.*]—it may, sir, I say, be necessary to obviate some objections that may be made to the motion; and first, it may be thought—I say, sir, some gentlemen may think, that this may prove pernicious to our manufacture—[*looks in his hat,*]—and the duty doubtless it is of every member of this illustrious assembly to have a particular eye unto that; but Mr. President—sir—[*looks in his hat, is confused, and sits down.*]

President. Mr. Twist, O pray finish, Mr. Twist.

Twist. [*Gets up.*] I say, Mr. President, that, sir, if, sir, it be considered that—as—I say—[*looks in his hat*]—I have nothing farther to say.

[*Sits down, and* Strap *gets up.*
President. Mr. Strap.

Strap. Mr. President, it was not my intention to trouble the assembly upon this occasion, but when I hear insinuations thrown out by gentlemen, where the interest of this country is so deeply concerned, I own I cannot sit silent; and give me leave to say, sir, there never came before this assembly a point of more importance than this; it strikes, sir, at the very root of your constitution; for, sir, what does this motion imply? it implies that porter, a wholesome, domestic manufacture, is to be prohibited at once. And for what, sir? for a foreign pernicious commodity. I had, sir, formerly the honour, in conjunction with my learned friend in the leather apron, to expel sherbet from amongst us, as I looked upon lemons as a fatal and foreign fruit; and can it be thought, sir, that I will sit silent to this? No, sir, I will put my shoulders strongly against it; I will oppose it *manibus totibus*. For should this proposal prevail, it will not end here: fatal, give me leave to say, will, I foresee, be the issue; and I shan't be surprised, in a few days, to hear from the same quarter, a motion for the expulsion of gin, and a premium for the importation of whisky.

[*A hum of approbation, with significant nods and winks from the other members. He sits down; and* Anvil *and another member get up together; some cry* Anvil, *others* Jacobs.

President. Mr. Anvil.

Anvil. Mr. President, sir—

[*The members all blow their noses, and cough;* Anvil *talks all the while, but is not heard.*

President. Silence, gentlemen; pray, gentlemen. A worthy member is up.

Anvil.

THE ORATORS.

Anvil. I fay Mr. Prefident, that if we confider this cafe in its utmoft extent—[*All the members cough, and blow their nofes again,*] —I fay, fir, I will. Nay, I infift on being heard. If any gentleman has any thing to fay any where elfe, I'll hear him.

[*Members all laugh, and* Anvil *fits down in a paffion, and* Slaughter *gets up.*]

Prefident. Mr. Samuel Slaughter.

Slaughter. Sir, I declare it, at the bare hearing of this here motion, I am all over in a fweat; for my part I can't think what gentlemen mean by talking in that there manner; not but I likes that every man fhould deliver his mind; I does mine; it has been ever my way; and when a member oppofes me I like him the better for it; it's right; I am pleafed; he can't pleafe me more; it is as it fhould be; and tho' I differ from the honourable gentleman in the flannel nightcap, over the way, yet I am pleafed to hear him fay what he thinks; for, fir, as I faid, it is always my rule to fay what I think, right or wrong—[*a loud laugh.*]—Ay, ay, gentlemen may laugh, with all my heart, I am ufed to it, I don't mind it a farthing ; but, fir, with regard to that there motion, I entirely agree with my worthy friend with the pewter-pot at his mouth. Now, fir, I would fain afk any gentleman this here queftion; Can any thing in nature be more natural for an

Englifhman,

Englishman, than porter? I declare, Mr. President, I think it the most wholesomest liquor in the world. But if it must be a change, let us change it for rum, a wholesome palatable liquor, a liquor that—in short, Mr. President, I don't know such a liquor. Ay, gentlemen may stare; I say, and I say it upon my conscience, I don't know such a liquor. Besides, I think there is in this here affair a point of law, which I shall leave to the consideration of the learned, and for that there reason, I shall take up no more of your time.

[*He sits down*, Catchpole *gets up.*
President. Mr. Catchpole.
Catchpole. I get up to the point of law. And though, sir, I am bred to the business, I can't say I am prepared for this question. But though this usquebagh, as a dram, may not (by name) be subject to a duty, yet, it is my opinion, or rather belief, it will be considered, as in the case of horses, to come under the article of dried goods—But I move that another day this point be debated.
Slaughter. I second the motion.
[Catchpole *gives a paper to the President who reads it.*
President. Hear your motion.
" That it be debated next Thursday, whe-
" ther the dram usquebagh is subject to a
" particular duty; or, as in the case of horses,
" to

"to be confidered under the article of dried goods."

All. Agreed, agreed.

Foote. And, now, ladies and gentlemen, having produced to you glaring proofs of our great ability in every fpecies of oratory, having manifefted, in the perfons of our pupils, our infinite addrefs in conveying our knowledge to others, we fhall clofe our morning's lecture, inftituted for public good, with a propofal for the particular improvement of individuals. We are ready to give private inftructions to any reverend gentleman in his probationary fermon for a lecturefhip; to young barrifters who have caufes to open, or motions to make; to all candidates of the fock or bufkin; or to the new members of any of thofe oratorical focieties with which this metropolis is at prefent fo plentifully ftocked.

[*Exeunt omnes.*

F I N I S.

PLAYS in 12mo. printed for W. LOWNDES,

At Sixpence each.

☞ *The Plays marked thus*, are either those which form* THE NEW ENGLISH THEATRE, *or are such as have been printed since that publication, in the same elegant manner.*

ABRAMULE, by Dr. Trapp
Adventures of Half an Hour, by Bullock
Agis, by Mr. Home
Albion and Albanius, by Dryden
Albion Queens, by Banks
Alchemist, by Ben Jonson
Alcibiades, by Otway
*All for Love, by Dryden
Amboyna, by Dryden
Amphitryon, by Dryden
*Amphitryon, altered by Dr. Hawkesworth
Anatomist, by Ravenscroft
Antony and Cleopatra, by Shakspeare
Arden of Feversham, Lillo
*Artaxerxes, by Dr. Arne
Artful Husband, Taverner
*Arthur and Emmeline
Artifice, by Mrs. Centlivre
*As you Like it, Shakspeare
Athaliah, by Duncombe
Aurengzebe, by Dryden
*Barbarossa, by Dr. Brown
Bartholomew Fair, Jonson
Basset Table, by Centlivre
*Beaux Stratagem, by Farquhar
*Beggar's Opera, by Gay
Biter, by Rowe
*Bold Stroke for a Wife, by Mrs. Centlivre
British Enchanters, by Lansdowne
*Brothers, by Dr. Young

Busiris, by Dr. Young
*Busy Body, by Centlivre
Cæsar in Egypt, by Cibber
*Carelefs Husband, ditto
Catiline, by Ben Jonson
*Cato, by Addison
Cheats of Scapin, Otway
Chances, by Buckingham
*Chances, by Garrick
Chaplet, by Moses Mendez
Cleomenes, by Dryden
Cobler of Preston, by Bullock
Comedy of Errors, by Shakspeare
Comical Lovers, by Cibber
*Committee, by Howard
*Confederacy, by Vanbrugh
Conquest of Granada, Dryden
*Conscious Lovers, by Steele
Constantine the Great, Lee
*Constant Couple, Farquhar
Contrivances, by H. Carey
*Coriolanus, by Shakspeare
Country Lasses, by Johnson
Country Wife, by Wycherley
*Country Wife, by Garrick
Country Wit, by Crown
*Cymbeline, by Garrick
Damon and Phillida, Dibdin
Devil of a Wife, by Jevon
Devil to Pay, by Coffey
*Distrest Mother, by Philips
Don Carlos, by Otway
*Double Dealer, Congreve
*Double Gallant, by Cibber
*Douglas, by Mr. Home
Dragon of Wantley, by Carey

PLAYS *printed for* W. LOWNDES.

*Drummer, by Addifon
Duke and no Duke, Cockain
Duke of Guife, by Dryden
Earl of Effex, by Banks
*Earl of Effex, by Jones
Earl of Warwick, by Franklin
Edward the Black Prince, by Shirley
Evening's Love, by Dryden
*Every Man in his Humour, by Garrick
*Fair Penitent, by Rowe
Fair Quaker of Deal, by C. Shadwell
Falfe Friends, by Vanbrugh
Fatal Secret, by Theobald
Flora, or Hob in the Well, by Hippifley
Fox, by Ben Jonfon
*Foundling, by Moore
Friendfhip in Fafhion, Otway
*Funeral, by Steele
Gamefter, by Centlivre
*Gamefter, by Mr. Moore
Gentle Shepherd, by Ramfay
*George Barnwell, by Lillo
Gil Blas, by Mr. Moore
Gloriana, by Lee
Great Favourite, by Howard
*Grecian Daughter, by Mr. Murphy
Greenwich Park, Mountfort
*Hamlet
*Henry IV. 2 parts
Henry V. ———
Henry VI. 3 parts
*Henry VIII.
} by Shakfpeare
Henry V. by Hill
Honeft Yorkfhireman, Carey
Humours of Purgatory, Griffin
*Hypocrite, by Bickerftaff
*Jane Gray, by Rowe
*Jane Shore, by Rowe
*Inconftant, by Farquhar
*Ifabella, by Garrick
Ifland Princefs, by Motteux
*Julius Cæfar, by Shakfpeare

King Charles I. by Havard
*King John, by Shakfpeare
*King Lear, by Garrick
King Lear, by Shakfpeare
King Lear, by Tate
Limberham, by Dryden
*Lionel and Clariffa, by Mr. Bickerftaff
Litigants, by Ozell
*Love for Love, Congreve
Love in a Mift, Cunningham
Love in a Tub, by Etherege
*Love makes a Man, C. Cibber
Love's Laft Shift, C. Cibber
*Love in a Village, Bickerftaff
Love's Labour Loft, Shakfpeare
Love Triumphant, by Dryden
Lying Lover, by Steele
*Macbeth, by Shakfpeare
*Mahomet, by Miller
*Maid of the Mill, Bickerftaff
Man of Mode, Etherege
Mariamne, by Fenton
Maffacre at Paris, by Lee
*Medea, by Mr. Glover
*Meafure for Meafure, by Shakfpeare
*Merchant of Venice, ditto
*Merope, by A. Hill
*Merry Wives of Windfor, by Shakfpeare
Miller of Mansfield, Dodfley
*Minor, by Foote
*Mifer, by Fielding
Miftake, by Vanbrugh
*Mourning Bride, Congreve
*Much ado about Nothing, by Shakfpeare
Muftapha, by Orrery
New Way to pay Old Debts, altered from Maffinger
Nonjuror, by C. Cibber
Oedipus, by Dryden
*Old Bachelor, by Congreve
*Orphan, by Otway
*Oroonoko, by Southern
*Othello, by Shakfpeare

PLAYS *printed for* W. LOWNDES.

Perjured Husband, Centlivre
Perolla and Izadora, Cibber
*Phædra and Hippolitus, by Smith
Philotas, by Frowde
Pilgrim, by Fletcher
Polly, by Gay
Prophetess, by Beaumont
*Provoked Husband, Cibber
*Provoked Wife, Vanbrugh
*Recruiting Officer, Farquhar
Rehearsal, by Buckingham
Relapse, by Vanbrugh
*Revenge, by Dr. Young
*Richard III. by Cibber
Rival Fools, by C. Cibber
Rival Ladies, by Dryden
*Rival Queens, altered
*Roman Father, Whitehead
*Romeo and Juliet, Garrick
Royal Merchant, Beaumont
*Rule a Wife, Beaumont
School-boy, by Cibber
Scornful Lady, Beaumont
*She would and she would not, by C. Cibber
She would if she could, by Etherege
*Siege of Damascus, Hughes
Siege of Aquileia, Home
Silent Woman, by Jonson
Sir Courtly Nice, by Crown
Sir Harry Wildair, Farquhar
Sir Martin Mar-All, Dryden
Sir Walter Raleigh, by Sewell
*Spanish Friar, by Dryden
Squire of Alsatia, by Shadwell
Stage Coach, by Farquhar
State of Innocence, by Dryden
Strollers, by Breval
*Suspicious Husband, by Dr. Hoadley
*Tamerlane, by Rowe
*Taming of the Shrew, by Garrick

*Tancred and Sigismunda, by Thomson
*Tempest, by Shakspeare
Tender Husband, by Steele
*Theodosius, by Lee
Timon of Athens, Shakspeare
Titus and Berenice, Otway
Toy Shop, by Dodsley
*Twelfth Night, Shakspeare
Twin Rivals, by Farquhar
Two Gentlemen of Verona, by Shakspeare
*Venice Preserved, by Otway
Venus and Adonis, by Cibber
Vestal Virgin, by Howard
Ulysses, by Rowe
*Way of the World, by Congreve
What d'ye call it ? by Gay
Wife's Relief, by Johnson
Wild Gallant, by Dryden
*Winter's Tale, by Garrick
Wit without Money, by Beaumont
Woman's a Riddle, by Bullock
Woman's Revenge, ditto
*Wonder, by Centlivre
Xerxes, by C. Cibber
*Zara, by Hill.

12*mo. at One Shilling each.*

Albumazar, by Tomkis
Eastward Hoe, by Chapman, Ben Jonson, &c.
Gentleman Dancing Master, by Wycherley
Love in a Wood, Wycherley
Miser, French and English, by Ozell
Mort d'Adam
Pasquin, by Fielding
Perkin Warbeck, by Ford
Plague of Riches, French and English, by Ozell

PLAYS *printed for* W. LOWNDES.

Tragedies, Comedies, and Operas,
In 8vo. at 1s. 6d. each.

Those distinguished by an Asterisk are embellished with Frontispieces.

ACHILLES, by Gay
Accomplished Maid, by Mr Toms
Agis, by Mr. Home
Albina, by Mrs. Cowley
All in the Wrong, Murphy
*Alzuma, by Murphy
*Amintas, by Tasso
Arminius, by Patterson
Astrologer, by Mr. Ralph
Athelstan, by Dr. Brown
Athelwold, by A. Hill
Author's Farce, by Fielding
Bankrupt, by Mr. Foote
Barbarossa, by Dr. Brown
Battle of Hastings, Cumberland
*Beggar's Opera, with music, by Gay
Bold Stroke for a Husband, by Mrs. Cowley
*Braganza, by Jephson
Brothers, by Cumberland
Brothers, by Young
Caractacus, by Mason
Carmelite, by Cumberland
Cælia, by C. Johnson
Chapter of Accidents, Miss Lee
Choleric Fathers, Holcroft
Choleric Man, Cumberland
Clandestine Marriage, by Garrick and Colman
Clementina, by Kelly
*Cleone, by Dodsley
Cleonice, by Mr. Hoole
Coffee-House Politician, by Fielding
Commissary, by Mr. Foote
Constantine, by Francis
Coquette, by Hitchcock
Coriolanus, by T. Sheridan
Count of Narbonne, Jephson
Countess of Salisbury, Hartson
Cozeners, by Mr. Foote

Creusa, by Mr. Whitehead
*Critic, by Mr. Sheridan
Cymbeline, by Hawkins
Cymon, by Mr. Garrick
Devil on Two Sticks, Foote
Disbanded Officer, Johnstone
Distressed Wife, by Gay
Douglas, by Mr. Home
Double Mistake, Mrs. Griffiths
Duellist, by Dr. Kenrick
Dupe, by Mrs. Sheridan
Duplicity, by Holcroft
Earl of Essex, by Jones
Earl of Essex, by Brooke
Elfred, by A. Hill
Elfrida, by Mr. Mason
Elvira, by Mr. Mallet
Emilia, by Mr. Meilan
English Merchant, Colman
Eugenia, by Mr. Francis
Eurydice, by Mr. Mallet
Fair Circassian, by Pratt
Fall of Mortimer, Wilkes, 2s.
*False Delicacy, by Kelly
Falstaff's Wedding, Dr. Kenrick
Fashionable Lover, Cumberland
Fate of Sparta, Mrs. Cowley
Fatal Vision, by A. Hill
Fathers, by Mr. Fielding
Follies of a Day, by Holcroft
Friends, by Mr. Meilan
Gil Blas, by Mr. Moore
*Goodnatured Man, Goldsmith
Grubstreet Opera, Fielding
Guardian outwitted, by Arne
Hecuba, by Dr. Delap
Heiress, by Gen. Burgoyne
*Henry VIII. by Grove
Heroine of the Cave, Jones
He would be a Soldier, Pilon
I'll tell you what, Mrs. Inchbald
Incle and Yarico, Colman, jun.
Insolvent, by A. Hill

PLAYS printed for W. LOWNDES.

Julia, by Mr. Jephfon
Lady's Revenge, Popple
Lame Lover, by Foote
Law of Lombardy, Jephfon
Ditto, on royal paper, 2s. 6d.
Love in a Riddle, with muſic, by Cibber
Love in feveral Mafques
Love in the Eaſt, by Cobb
Lyar, by Foote
*Magic Picture, by Bate
Mahomet, by Garrick
*Maid of the Mill, Bickerſtaff
Maid of Bath, by Foote
Man and Wife, by Colman
Man of Bufinefs, by ditto
Married Coquet, by Baillie
Methodiſt, by Pottinger
Midas, by Mr. O'Hara
*Minor, by Foote
Modern Huſband, Fielding
Momus turned Fabuliſt
More Ways than one, by Mrs. Cowley
Mother-in-Law, by Miller
Muſtapha, by Mallet
Myſterious Huſband, by Cumberland
Nabob, by Foote
Natural Son, by Cumberland
New Peerage, by Miſs Lee
Noble Peaſant, by Holcroft
Northumberland, by Meilan
Oliver Cromwell, by Green
Orators, by Foote
Orphan of China, Murphy
Pafquin, by Fielding
Patron, by Foote
Percy, by Miſs More
Periander, by Atkins
Philoclea, by Mr. Morgan
*Plain Dealer, Bickerſtaff
Platonic Wife, by Griffiths
Refufal, by C. Cibber
Regulus, by Mr. Havard
Reparation, by Andrews
Richard Cœur de Lion, by Mr. Macnally

Rivals, by Mr. Sheridan
Robin Hood, by Macnally
Roman Father, Whitehead
Royal Merchant, by Hull
Royal Suppliants, by Delap
Scanderbeg, by Havard
School for Grey Beards, by Cowley
School for Guardians, Murphy
School for Lovers, Whitehead
School for Rakes, Mrs.Griffiths
*School for Wives, Kelly
Seduction, by Holcroft
Semiramis, by Voltaire
Sethona, by Col. Dow
She Stoops to Conquer, Goldfm.
Siege of Aquileia, by Home
Siege de Calais, par Belloy
Silvia, by Lillo
Siſter, by Mrs. Lenox
*Strangers at Home, by Cobb
Student, altered from Shakfp.
Such Things are, Mrs. Inchbald
Summer's Tale, Cumberland
Temple Beau, Fielding
Themiſtocles, by Madden
Timanthes, by Hoole
Times, by Mrs. Griffiths
Timon of Athens, altered by Cumberland
Timon in Love, by J. Kelly
Ton, by Lady Wallace
Trip to Calais, &c. Foote, 2s 6d
Trip to Scarborough, Sheridan
Village Opera, Johnfon
Virginia, by Mr. Crifpe
Virgin Queen, by Barford
Univerfal Gallant, Fielding
Univerfal Paffion, by Miller
Way to keep Him, Murphy
Weſt Indian, by Cumberland
Which is the Man; Mrs.Cowley
Widowed Wife, by Kenrick
Widow and no Widow, Jodrell
Word to the Wife, by Kelly
Zenobia, by Mr. Murphy
Zingis, by Col. Dow
Zoraida, by Mr. Hodfon

The MINOR.

THE

MINOR,

A

COMEDY.

WRITTEN BY

SAMUEL FOOTE, Esq.

AS IT IS ACTED AT THE

Theatre-Royal in Drury-Lane.

Tantam Religio potuit suadere Malorum.

THE TENTH EDITION.

LONDON:
Printed for T. Becket, Pall-Mall; W. Nicoll, St. Paul's Church-Yard; S. Bladon, Paternoster-Row; and W. Lowndes, Fleetstreet.

1789.

[Price One Shilling and Sixpence.]

Persons in the INTRODUCTION.

FOOTE,
CANKER,
SMART,
PEARSE,

In the COMEDY.

Sir William Wealthy,	Mr. BADDELEY.
Mr. Richard Wealthy,	Mr. WRIGHTEN.
Sir George Wealthy,	Mr. AICKIN.
Shift,	Mr. BANNISTER.
Loader,	Mr. BRANSBY.
Dick,	Mr. BURTON,
Transfer,	Mr. PARSONS.
Smirk,	Mr. BANNISTER.
The Baron assum'd,	Mr. BADDELEY.
Mrs. Cole,	Mr. BANNISTER.
Lucy,	Miss HOPKINS.

TO HIS GRACE

WILLIAM Duke of DEVONSHIRE,

Lord Chamberlain of his Majesty's Houshold,

MY LORD,

THE MINOR, who is indebted for his appearance on the stage to your Grace's indulgence, begs leave to desire your further protection, at his entering into the world.

Though the allegiance due from the whole dramatic people to your Grace's station, might place this address in the light of a natural tribute; yet, my Lord, I should not have taken that liberty with the Duke of Devonshire, if I could not at the same time, plead some little utility in the design of my piece; and add, that the public approbation has stamped a value on the execution.

The law, which threw the stage under the absolute government of a lord chamberlain, could not fail to fill the minds of all the objects of that power with very gloomy apprehensions; they found themselves (through their own licentiousness, it must be confess'd) in a more precarious dependent state, than any other of his Majesty's subjects. But when their direction was lodged in the hands of a nobleman, whose ancestors had so successfully struggled for national liberty, they ceased to fear for their own. It was not from a patron of the liberal arts they were to expect an oppressor; it was not from the friend of freedom, and of man, they were to dread partial monopolies, or the establishment of petty tyrannies.

Their

Their warmest wishes are accomplished; none of their rights have been invaded, except what, without the first poetic authority, I should not venture to call a right, the Jus Nocendi.

Your tenderness, my Lord, for all the followers of the Muses, has been in no instance more conspicuous, than in your late favour to me, the meanest of their train; your Grace has thrown open (for those who are denied admittance into the palaces of Parnassus) a cottage on its borders, where the unhappy migrants may be, if not magnificently, at least, hospitably entertained.

I shall detain your Grace no longer, than just to echo the public voice, that, for the honour, progress, and perfection of letters, your Grace may long continue their candid CENSOR, who have always been their generous protector.

I have the honour, my Lord, to be, with the greatest respect, and gratitude,

Your Grace's most dutiful,

most obliged,

and obedient Servant,

SAMUEL FOOTE,

Ellestre,
July 8, 1789.

THE

MINOR,

INTRODUCTION.

Enter CANKER *and* SMART.

SMART.

BUT are you sure he has leave?
Cank. Certain.
Smart. I'am damn'd glad on't. For now we shall have a laugh either with him, or at him, it does not signify which.
Cank. Not a farthing.
Smart. Do you know his scheme?
Cank. Not I. But is not the door of the Little Theatre open.

THE MINOR.

Smart. Yes. Who is that fellow that seems to stand centry there?

Cank. By his tatter'd garb and meagre visage, he must be one of the troop.

Smart. I'll call him. Holo, Mr.——

Enter PEARSE.

What, is there any thing going on over the way?

Pear. A rehearsal.

Smart. Of what?

Pear. A new piece.

Smart. Foote's?

Pear. Yes.

Cank. Is he there?

Pear. He is.

Smart. Zounds, let's go and see what he's about.

Cank. With all my heart.

Smart. Come along then. [*Exeunt.*

Enter FOOTE *and an* ACTOR.

Foote. Sir, this will never do? you must get rid of your high notes, and country cant. Oh, 'tis the true strolling.——

Enter SMART *and* CANKER.

Smart. Ha, ha, ha! what, hard at it, my boy!——Here's your old friend Canker and
I come

I come for a peep, Well, and hey, what is your plan?

Foote. Plan?

Smart. Ay, what are your characters? Give us your groupe; how is your cloth fill'd?

Foote. Characters!

Smart. Ay.—Come, come, communicate. What, man, we will lend thee a lift. I have a damn'd fine original for thee, an aunt of my own, juft come from the North, with the true Newcaftle bur in her throat; and a nofe and a chin.—I am afraid fhe is not well enough known: but I have a remedy for that. I'll bring her the firft night of your piece, place her in a confpicuous ftation, and whifper the fecret to the whole houfe. That will be damn'd fine, won't it?

Foote. Oh, delicious!

Smart. But don't name me. For if fhe fmokes me for the author, I fhall be dafh'd out of her codicil in a hurry.

Foote. Oh, never fear me. But I fhou'd think your uncle Tom a better character.

Smart. What the politician?

Foote. Aye; that every day, after dinner, as foon as the cloth is remov'd, fights the battle of Minden, batters the French with cherry-ftones, and purfues 'em to the banks of the Rhine in a ftream of fpilt port.

Smart. Oh, damn it, he'll do.

Foote.

Foote. Or what say you to your father-in-law, Sir Timothy ? who, tho' as broken-winded as a Hounslow post-horse, is eternally chaunting Venetian ballads. Kata tore cara higlia.

Smart. Admirable ! by heavens !— Have you got 'em.

Foote. No.

Smart. Then in with 'em my boy.

Foote. Not one.

Smart. Pr'ythee why not ?

Foote. Why look'e, Smart, though you are, in the language of the world, my friend, yet there is one thing you, I am sure, love better than any body.

Smart. What's that ?

Foote. Mischief.

Smart. No, pr'ythee.

Foote. How now am I sure that you, who so readily give up your relations, may not have some design upon me ?

Smart. I don't understand you.

Foote. Why, as soon as my characters begin to circulate a little successfully, my mouth is stopp'd in a minute, by the clamour of your relations,——Oh, damme,—'tis a shame,—it should not be,—people of distinction brought upon the stage.—And so out of compliment to your cousins, I am to be beggar'd for treating the public with the follies of your family, at your own request.

Smart,

Smart. How can you think I would be such a dog? What the devil, then, are we to have nothing personal? Give us the actors however.

Foote. Oh that's stale. Besides, I think they have of all men, the best right to complain.

Smart. How so?

Foote. Because, by rendering them ridiculous in their profession, you at the same time, injure their pockets. Now as to the other gentry, they have providentially something besides their understanding to rely on; and the only injury they can receive is, that the whole town is then diverted with what before, was only the amusement of private parties.

Canker. Give us then a national portrait: a Scotchman or an Irishman.

Foote. If you mean merely the dialect of the two countries, I can't think it either a subject of satire or humour; it is an accidental unhappiness, for which a man is no more accountable, than the colour of his hair. Now affectation I take to be the true comic object. If, indeed, a North Briton, struck with a scheme of reformation, should advance from the banks of the Tweed, to teach the English the true pronunciation of their own language, he would, I think, merit your laughter: nor would a Dublin mechanic, who, from heading the Liberty-boys

boys in a skirmish on Ormond Quay, should think he had a right to prescribe military laws to the first commander in Europe, be a less ridiculous object.

Smart. Are there such?

Foote. If you mean that the blunders of a few peasants, or the partial principles of a single scoundrel, are to stand as characteristical marks of a whole country; your pride may produce a laugh, but, believe me, it is at the expence of your understanding.

Canker. Heyday, what a system is here! Laws for laughing! And pray, sage Sir, instruct us when we may laugh with propriety?

Foote. At an old beau, a superannuated beauty, a military coward, a stuttering orator, or a gouty dancer. In short, whoever affects to be what he is not, or strives to be what he cannot, is an object worthy the poet's pen, and your mirth.

Smart. Psha, I don't know what you mean by your is nots, and cannots—damn'd abstruse jargon, Ha, Canker!

Cank. Well, but if you will not give us persons, let us have things. Treat us with a modern amour, and a state intrigue, or a———

Foote. And so amuse the public ear at the expence of private peace. You must excuse me.

Cank. And with these principles, you expect to thrive on this spot?

Smart

Smart. No, no, it won't do. I tell thee the plain roast and boil'd of the theatres will never do at this table. We must have high seaſon'd ragouts, and rich ſauces.

Foote. Why, perhaps, by way of deſert, I may produce ſomething that may hit your palate.

Smart. Your bill of fare?

Foote. What think you of one of thoſe itinerant field orators, who, tho' at declar'd enmity with common ſenſe, have the addreſs to poiſon the principles, and at the ſame time pick the pockets, of half our induſtrious fellow ſubjects?

Cank. Have a care. Dangerous ground, Ludere cum ſacris, you know.

Foote. Now I look upon it in a different manner. I conſider theſe gentlemen in the light of public performers, like myſelf; and whether we exhibit at Tottenham-court, or the Haymarket, our purpoſe is the ſame, and the place is immaterial.

Cank. Why, indeed if it be conſidered—

Foote. Nay, more, I muſt beg leave to aſſert, that ridicule is the only antidote againſt this pernicious poiſon. This is a madneſs that argument can never cure: and ſhould a little wholeſome ſeverity be applied, perſecution would be the immediate cry; where then can we have recourſe, but to the comic muſe, perhaps the archneſs and ſeverity of

her

her smile may redress an evil, that the laws cannot reach, or reason reclaim.

Cank. Why, if it does not cure those already distemper'd, it may be a means to stop the infection.

Smart. But how is your scheme conducted?

Foote. Of that you may judge. We are just going upon a repetition of the piece. I should be glad to have your opinion.

Smart. We will give it you.

Foote. One indulgence: As you are Englishmen, I think, I need not beg, that as from necessity most of my performers are new, you will allow for their inexperience, and encourage their timidity.

Smart. But reasonable.

Foote. Come, then, prompter, begin.

Pear. Lord, Sir, we are all at a stand.

Foote. What's the matter?

Pear. Mrs. O-Schohnesy has return'd the part of the bawd; she says she is a gentlewoman, and it would be a reflection on her family to do any such thing!

Foote. Indeed.

Pear. If it had been only a whore, says she, I should not have minded it; because no lady need be ashamed of doing that.

Foote. Well, there is no help for it; but these gentlemen must not be disappointed. Well, I'll do the character myself.

ACT I.

Sir WILLIAM WEALTHY, *and Mr.* RICH-
ARD WEALTHY.

Sir WILLIAM.

COME, come, brother, I know the world. People who have their attention eternally fixed upon one object, can't help being a little narrow in their notions.

R. Weal. A sagacious remark that, and highly probable, that we merchants, who maintain a constant correspondence with the four quarters of the world, should know less of it than your fashionable fellows, whose whole experience is bounded by Westminster-bridge.

Sir *Will.* Nay, brother, as a proof that I am not blind to the benefit of travelling, George, you know, has been in Germany these four years.

R. Weal. Where he is well grounded in gaming and gluttony; France has furnished him with fawning and flattery; Italy equip'd him with capriols and cantatas: and thus accomplish'd

complish'd, my young gentleman is return'd with a cargo of whores, cooks, valets de chambre, and fiddlesticks, a most valuable member of the British commonwealth.

Sir *Will.* You dislike then my system of education?

R. Weal. Most sincerely.

Sir *Will.* The whole?

R. Weal. Every particular.

Sir *Will.* The early part, I should imagine, might merit your approbation.

R. Weal. Least of all. What, I suppose, because he has run the gauntlet thro' a public school, where, at sixteen, he had practis'd more vices than he would otherwise have heard of at sixty.

Sir *Will.* Ha, ha, prejudice!

R. Weal. Then, indeed, you remov'd him to the university; where, left his morals should be mended, and his understanding improv'd, you fairly set him free from the restraint of the one, and the drudgery of the other, by the privileg'd distinction of a silk gown and a velvet cap.

Sir *Will.* And all these evils, you think, a city education would have prevented?

R. Weal. Doubtless.———Proverbs, proverbs, brother William, convey wholesome instruction. Idleness is the root of all evil. Regular hours, constant employment, and good example, can't fail to form the mind.

Sir

THE MINOR. 17

Sir *Will.* Why, truly, brother, had you stuck to your old civic vices, hypocrify, cozenage, and avarice, I don't know whether I might not have committed George to your care; but you cockneys now beat us suburbians at our own weapons. What, old boy, times are chang'd since the date of thy indentures; when the sleek, crop-eared prentice used to dangle after his mistress, with the great bible under his arm, to St. Bride's, on a Sunday; bring home the text, repeat the divisions of the discourse, dine at twelve, and regale, upon a gaudy day, with buns and beer at Islington, or Mile-End.

R. Weal. Wonderfully facetious!

Sir *Will.* Our modern lads are of a different metal. They have their gaming clubs in the Garden, their little lodgings, the snug depositories of their rusty swords, and occasional bag-wigs; their horses for the turf; ay, and their commissions of bankruptcy too, before they are well out of their time.

R. Weal. Infamous aspersion!

Sir *Will.* But the last meeting at Newmarket, lord Lofty received at the hazard-table the identical note from the individual taylor to whom he had paid it but the day before, for a new set of liveries.

R. Weal. Invention!

Sir *Will.* These are anecdotes you will never meet with in your weekly travels from
C   Cateaton-

Cateaton-ſtreet to your boarded box in Clapham, brother.

R. Wealth. And yet that boarded box, as your prodigal ſpendthrift proceeds, will ſoon be the only ſeat of the family.

Sir *Will.* May be not. Who knows what a reformation our project may produce!

R. Wealth. I do. None at all.

Sir *Will.* Why ſo?

R. Wealth. Becauſe your means are ill-proportion'd to their end. Were he my ſon, I would ſerve him——

Sir *Will.* As you have done your daughter. Diſcard him. But conſider, I have but one.

R. Wealth. That would weigh nothing with me: for, was Charlotte to ſet up a will of her own, and reject the man of my choice, ſhe muſt expect to ſhare the fate of her ſiſter. I conſider families as a ſmaller kind of kingdoms, and would have diſobedience in the one as ſeverely puniſhed as rebellion in the other. Both cut off from their reſpective ſocieties.

Sir *Will.* Poor Lucy! But ſurely you begin to relent. Mayn't I intercede?

R. Wealth. Look'e, brother, you know my mind. I will be abſolute. If I meddle with the management of your ſon, it is at your own requeſt; but if, directly or indirectly, you interfere with my baniſhment of that wilful, headſtrong, diſobedient huſſy,

all

all ties between us are broke; and I shall no more remember you as a brother, than I do her as a child.

Sir *Will.* I have done. But to return. You think there is a probability in my plan?

R. Wealth. I shall attend the issue.

Sir *Will.* You will lend your aid, however?

R. Wealth. We shall see how you go on.

Enter SERVANT.

Serv. A letter, sir.

Sir *Will.* Oh, from Capias, my attorney. Who brought it?

Serv. The person is without, sir.

Sir *Will.* Bid him wait. [*Reads.*] [*Exit. Serv.*

Worthy Sir,

The bearer is the person I promised to procure. I thought it was proper for you to examine him in viva voce. So if you administer a few interrogatories, you will find, by cross-questioning him, whether he is a competent person to prosecute the cause you wot of. I wish you a speedy issue: and as there can be no default in your judgment, am of opinion it should be carried into immediate execution. I am,

Worthy Sir, &c.

TIMOTHY CAPIAS.

P. S.

P. S. *The party's Name is* Samuel Shift. *He is an admirable mime, or mimic, and moſt delectable company; as we experience every Tueſday night at our club, the Magpye and Horſe-ſhoe, Fetter-lane.*

Very methodical indeed, Mr. Capias!—John.

Enter SERVANT.

Bid the perſon who brought this Letter, walk in. [*Exit.* Serv.] Have you any curioſity, brother?
R. Wealth. Not a jot. I muſt to the Change. In the evening you may find me in the counting-houſe, or at Jonathan's.
[*Exit* R. Wealthy.
Sir *Will.* You ſhall hear from me.

Enter SHIFT *and* SERVANT.

Shut the door, John, and remember, I am not at home. [*Exit* Serv.] You came from Mr. Capias?
Shift. I did, ſir.
Sir *Will.* Your name I think, is Shift?
Shift. It is, ſir.
Sir *Will.* Did Mr. Capias drop any hint of my buſineſs with you?
Shift. None. He only ſaid, with his ſpectacles on his noſe, and his hand upon his chin, Sir William Wealthy is a reſpectable perſonage, and my client; he wants to re-
tain

tain you in a certain affair, and will open the cafe, and give you your brief himfelf: if you adhere to his inftructions, and carry your caufe, he is generous, and will difcharge your bill without taxation.

Sir *Will.* Ha! ha! my friend Capias to a hair! Well, fir, this is no bad fpecimen of your abilities. But fee that the door is faft. Now, fir, you are to―――

Shift. A moment's paufe, if you pleafe. You muft know, Sir William, I am a prodigious admirer of forms. Now Mr. Capias tells me, that it is always the rule, to adminifter a retaining fee before you enter upon the merits.

Sir *Will.* Oh, fir, I beg your pardon!

Shift. Not that I queftion'd your generofity; but forms you know―――

Sir *Will.* No apology, I beg. But as we are to have a clofer connection, it may not be amifs, by way of introduction, to underftand one another a little. Pray, fir, where was you born?

Shift. At my father's.

Sir *Will.* Hum?―――And what was he?

Shift. A gentleman.

Sir *Will.* What was you bred?

Shift. A gentleman.

Sir *Will.* How do you live?

Shift. Like a gentleman.

Sir *Will.* Cou'd nothing induce you to unbofom yourfelf?

Shift.

Shift. Look'e, Sir William, there is a kind of fomething in your countenance, a certain opennefs and generofity, a je ne fcai quoi in your manner, that I will unlock: You fhall fee me all.

Sir *Will.* You will oblige me.

Shift. You muft know then, that Fortune, which frequently delights to raife the nobleft ftructures from the fimpleft foundations; who from a taylor made a pope, from a gin-fhop an emprefs, and many a prime minifter from nothing at all, has thought fit to raife me to my prefent height, from the humble employment of—Light your Honour——A link boy.

Sir *Will.* A pleafant fellow.——Who were your parents;

Shift. I was produced, fir, by a left-handed marriage, in the language of the news-papers, between an illuftrious lamp-lighter and an eminent itinerant cat and dog butcher.—Cat's meat, and dog's meat. ——I dare fay, you have heard my mother fir. But as to this happy pair I owe little befides my being, I fhall drop them where they dropt me——in the ftreet.

Sir *Will.* Proceed.

Shift. My firft knowledge of the world I owe to a fchool, which has produced many a great man; the avenues of the Play-houfe. There, fir, leaning on my extinguifh'd link, I learn'd dexterity from pick-pockets, con-

nivance

nivance from conſtables, politics and faſhions from footmen, and the art of making and breaking a promiſe, from their maſters. Here, ſirrah, light me a-croſs the kennel. ——I hope your honour will remember poor Jack.——You ragged raſcal, I have no half-pence——I'll pay you the next time I ſee you——But, lack-a-day, ſir, that time I ſaw as ſeldom as his tradeſmen.

Sir *Will.* Very well.

Shift. To theſe accompliſhments from without the Theatre, I muſt add one that I obtain'd within.

Sir *Will.* How did you gain admittance there?

Shift. My merit, ſir, that, like my link, threw a radiance round me——A detachment from the head-quarters here, took poſſeſſion, in the ſummer, of a country corporation, where I did the honours of the barn, by ſweeping the ſtage, and clipping the candles. There my ſkill and addreſs was ſo conſpicuous, that it procur'd me the ſame office the enſuing winter, at Drury-Lane, where I acquir'd intrepidity; the crown of all my virtues.

Sir *Will.* How did you obtain that?

Shift. By my poſt. For I think, ſir, he that dares ſtand the ſhot of the gallery in lighting, ſnuffing, and ſweeping, the firſt night of a new play, may bid defiance to the pillory, with all its cuſtomary compliments.

Sir Will. Some truth in that.

Shift. But an unlucky crab-apple, apply'd to my right eye, by a patriot gingerbread-baker from the Borough, who would not fuffer three dancers from Switzerland, be-caufe he hated the French, forced me to a precipitate retreat.

Sir Will. Poor devil?

Shift. Broglio and Contades have done the fame. But as it happend, like a tennis-ball, I rofe higher than the rebound.

Sir Will. How fo?

Shift. My misfortune, fir, mov'd the com-paffion of one of our performers, a whimfi-cal man, he took me into his fervice. To him I owe, what I believe, will make me ufeful to you.

Sir Will. Explain.

Shift. Why, fir, my mafter was remark-ably happy in an art, which, however difef-teem'd at prefent, is, by Tully, reckon'd amongft the perfections of an orator; Mi-mickry.

Sir Will. Why, you are deeply read Mr. Shift!

Shift. A fmattering—But as I was faying, fir, nothing came amifs to my mafter. Bi-peds, or quadrupeds; rationals, or animals; from the clamour of the bar, to the cackle of the barn-door; from the foporific twang of the tabernacle of Tottenham-Court, to the melodious bray of their long ear'd bre-
thren

thren in Bunhill-Fields; all were objects of his imitation, and my attention. In a word, fir, for two whole years, under this professor, I study'd and starv'd, impoverish'd my body, and pamper'd my mind; till thinking myself pretty near equal to my master, I made him one of his own bows, and set up for myself.

Sir *Will.* You have been succefsful, I hope.

Shift. Pretty well, I can't complain. My art, fir, is a pafs-par-tout. I feldom want employment. Let's fee how stand my engagements. [*Pulls out a pocket-book*] Hum, —hum, Oh! Wednefday at Mrs. Gammut's near Hanover-fquare; there, there, I shall make a meal upon the Mingotti; for her ladyship is in the opera intereft; but, however, I shall revenge her caufe upon her rival Mattei, Sunday evening at Lady Suſtinuto's concert. Thurfday I dine upon the actors, with ten Templars, at the Mitre in Fleet-ftreet. Friday I am to give the amorous parly of two intriguing cats in a gutter, with the disturbing of a hen-rooft, at Mr. Deputy Sugarfops, near the Monument. So fir, you fee my hands are full. In fhort, Sir William, there is not a buck or a turtle devoured within the bills of mortality, but there I may, if I pleafe, ftick a napkin under my chin.

Sir

Sir *Will.* I'm afraid, Mr. Shift, I muſt break in a little upon your engagements; but you ſhall be no loſer by the bargain.

Shift. Command me.

Sir *Will.* You can be ſecret as well as ſerviceable?

Shift. Mute as a mackrel.

Sir *Will.* Come hither then. If you betray me to my ſon.——

Shift. Scalp me.

Sir *Will.* Enough.—You muſt know then, the hopes of our family are, Mr. Shift, center'd in one boy.

Shift. And I warrant, he is a hopeful one.

Sir *Will.* No interruption, I beg. George has been abroad theſe four years, and from his late behaviour, I have reaſon to believe, that had a certain event happened, which I am afraid he wiſhed,—my death———

Shift. Yes; that's natural enough.

Sir *Will.* Nay, pray,—there wou'd ſoon be an end to an ancient and honourable family.

Shift. Very melancholy indeed. But families, like beſoms. will wear to the ſtumps, and finally fret out, as you ſay.

Sir *Will.* Pr'ythee peace for five minutes.

Shift. I am tongue-ty'd.

Sir *Will.* Now I have projected a ſcheme to prevent this calamity.

Shift, Ay, I ſhould be glad to hear that.

Sir *Will.* I am going to tell it you.

Shift. Proceed.

Sir

Sir *Will.* George, as I have contrived it, shall experience all the misery of real ruin without running the least risque.

Shift. Ay, that will be a coup de maitre.

Sir *Will.* I have prevail'd upon his uncle, a wealthy citizen.——

Shift. I don't like a city plot.

Sir *Will.* I tell thee it is my own.

Shift. I beg pardon.

Sir *Will.* My brother, I say, some time since wrote him a circumstantial account of my death; upon which, he is returned, in full expectation of succeeding to my estate.

Shift. Immediately.

Sir *Will.* No; when at age. In about three months.

Shift. I understand you.

Sir *Will.* Now, sir, guessing into what hands my heedless boy would naturally fall, on his return, I have, in a feign'd character, associated myself with a set of rascals, who will spread every bait that can flatter folly, inflame extravagance, allure inexperience, or catch credulity. And when, by their means, he thinks himself reduc'd to the last extremity; lost even to the most distant hope——

Shift. What then?

Sir *Will.* Then will I step in like his guardian-angel, and snatch him from perdition. If mortify'd by misery, he becomes conscious of his errors, I have sav'd my son;
but

but if, on the other hand, gratitude can't bind, nor ruin reclaim him, I will caſt him out, as an alien to my blood, and truſt for the ſupport of my name and family to a remoter branch.

Shift. Bravely reſolv'd. But what part am I to ſuſtain in this drama?

Sir *Will.* Why George, you are to know, is already ſtript of what money he could command, by two ſharpers; but as I never truſt them out of my ſight they can't deceive me.

Shift. Out of your ſight!

Sir *Will.* Why, I tell thee, I am one of the knot; an adept in their ſcience, can ſlip, ſhuffle, cog, or cut with the beſt of 'em.

Shift. How do you eſcape your ſon's notice?

Sir *Will.* His firm perſuaſion of my death, with the extravagance of my diſguiſe.—— Why, I wou'd engage to elude your penetration, when I am beau'd out for the baron. But of that by and by. He has recourſe, after his ill ſucceſs, to the cent. per cent. gentry, the uſurers, for a further ſupply.

Shift, Natural enough.

Sir *Will.* Pray do you know,—I forgot his name,—a wrinkled old fellow, in a thread-bare coat? He ſits every morning, from twelve till two, in the left corner of Lloyd's coffee-houſe; and every evening, from
five

five till eight, under the clock, at the Temple-exchange.

Shift. What, little Transfer the broker!

Sir *Will.* The fame. Do you know him?

Shift. Know him! Ay, rot him. It was but laft Eafter Tuefday, he had me turn'd out at a feaft, in Leather-feller's Hall, for finging Room for Cuckold's, like a parrot; and vow'd it meant a reflection upon the whole body corporate.

Sir *Will.* You have reafon to remember him.

Shift. Yes, yes, I recommended a minor to him myfelf, for the loan only of fifty pounds; and wou'd you believe it, as I hope to be fav'd, we din'd, fupp'd, and wetted five-and-thirty guineas upon tick, in meetings at the Crofs-keys, in order to fettle the terms; and after all, the fcoundrel would not lend us a ftiver.

Sir *Will.* Cou'd you perfonate him?

Shift. Him! Oh, you fhall fee me fhift into his fhamble in a minute: and, with a wither'd face, a bit of a purple nofe, a cautionary ftammer, and a fleek filver head, I would undertake to deceive even his banker. But to fpeak the truth, I have a friend that can do this inimitably well. Have not you fomething of more confequence for me?

Sir *Will.* I have. Cou'd not you, mafter Shift, affume another fhape? You have attended auctions.

Shift.

Shift. Auctions! a conſtant puff. Deep in the myſtery; a profeſſed conoiſſeur, from a Niger to a nautilus, from the Apollo Belvidere to a butterfly.

Sir *Will.* One of theſe inſinuating, oily orators I will get you to perſonate: for we muſt have the plate and jewels in our poſſeſſion, or they will ſoon fall into other hands.

Shift. I will do it.

Sir *Will.* Within I'll give you farther inſtructions.

Shift. I'll follow you.

Sir *Will.* [*Going, returns.*] You will want materials.

Shift. Oh, my dreſs I can be furniſh'd with in five minutes. [*Exit Sir* Will.] A whimſical old blade this. I ſhall laugh if this ſcheme miſcarries. I have a ſtrange mind to lend it a lift—never had a greater—Pho, a damn'd unnatural connection this of mine! What have I to do with fathers and guardians! a parcel of preaching, prudent, careful, curmudgeonly——dead to pleaſures themſelves, and the blaſters of it in others ——Mere dogs in a manger—No, no, I'll veer, tack about, open my budget to the boy, and join in a counter-plot. But hold, hold, friend Stephen, ſee firſt how the land lies. Who knows whether this Germaniz'd genius has parts to comprehend, or ſpirit to reward thy merit. There's danger in that, aye,

aye, marry is there. 'Egad before I shift the helm, I'll first examine the coast; and then if there be but a bold shore, and a good bottom, have a care old Square Toes, you will meet with your match. [*Exit*.

Enter Sir GEORGE, LOADER, *and Servant.*

Sir *Geo*. Let the Martin pannels for the vis-a-vis be carried to Long-Acre, and the pye-balls sent to Hall's to be bitted——You will give me leave to be in your debt till the evening, Mr. Loader. I have just enough left to discharge the baron; and we must, you know, be punctual with him, for the credit of the country.

Load. Fire him, a snub-nos'd son of a bitch. Levant me, but he got enough last night to purchase a principality amongst his countrymen, the High-dutchians and Huffarians.

Sir *Geo*. You had your share, Mr. Loader.

Load. Who, I! Lurch me at four, but I was mark'd to the top of your trick, by the baron, my dear. What, I am no cinque and quarter man. Come, shall we have a dip in the history of the Four Kings this morning?

Sir *Geo*. Rather too early. Besides, it is the rule abroad, never to engage a-fresh, till our old scores are discharg'd.

Load.

Load. Capot me, but thofe lads abroad are pretty fellows, let'em fay what they will. Here, fir, they will vowel you, from father to fon, to the twentieth generation. They wou'd as foon now-a-days pay a tradefman's bill, as a play debt. All fenfe of honour is gone, not a ftiver ftirring. They cou'd as foon raife the dead as two pounds two; nick me, but I have a great mind to tie up, and ruin the rafcals—What, has Transfer been here this morning?

Enter DICK.

Sir *Geo.* Any body here this morning, Dick?
Dick. No body, your honour.
Load. Repique the rafcal. He promis'd to be here before me.
Dick. I beg your honour's pardon. Mrs. Cole from the Piazza was here, between feven and eight.
Sir *Geo.* An early hour for a lady of her calling.
Dick. Mercy on me! The poor gentlewoman is mortally altered fince we us'd to lodge there, in our jaunts from Oxford; wrapt up in flannels: all over the rheumatife.
Load. Ay, ay, old Moll is at her laft ftake.
Dick.

THE MINOR.

Dick. She bade me fay, fhe juft ftopt in her way to the tabernacle; after the exhortations, fhe fays, fhe'll call again.

Sir *Geo.* Exhortation! Oh, I recollect. Well, whilft they only make profelytes from that profeffion, they are heartily welcome to them.—She does not mean to make me a convert?

Dick. I believe fhe has fome fuch defign upon me; for fhe offer'd me a book of hymns, a fhilling, and a dram, to go along with her.

Sir *Geo.* No bad fcheme, Dick. Thou haft a fine fober, pfalm-finging countenance; and when thou haft been fome time in their trammels, may make as able a teacher as the beft of 'em.

Dick. Laud, fir, I want learning.

Sir *Geo.* Oh, the fpirit, the fpirit will fupply all that, Dick, never fear.

Enter Sir WILLIAM *as a German Baron.*

My dear baron, what news from the Haymarket? What fays the Florenza? Does fhe yield? Shall I be happy? Say yes, and command my fortune.

Sir *Will.* I was never did fee fo fine a woman fince I was leave Hamburgh; dere was all de colour, all red and white, dat was quite natural; point d'artifice. Then fhe was dance and fing—I vow to heaven, I was never fee de like!

D   Sir

Sir *Geo.* But how did she receive my embassy? What hopes?

Sir *Will.* Why dere was, monsieur le chevalier, when I first enter, dree or four damn'd queer people? ah, ah, dought I, by gad I guess your business. Dere was one fat big woman's, dat I know long time: le valet de chambre was tell me dat she came from a grand merchand; ha, ha, dought I, by your leave, stick to your shop; or, if you must have de pritty girl, dere is de play-hous, dat do very well for you; but for de opera, pardonnez, by gar dat is meat for your master.

Sir *Geo.* Insolent mechanic!—but she despis'd him?

Sir *Will.* Ah, may foy, he is damn'd rich, has beaucoup de guineas; but after de fat woman was go, I was tell the signora, madam, der is one certain chevalier of dis country, who has travell'd, see de world, bien fait, well made, beaucoup d'Esprit; a great deal of monies, who beg, by gar, to have de honour to drow himself at your feet.

Sir *Geo.* Well, well, barón.

Sir *Will.* She aska your name; as soon as I tell her, aha, by gar, dans an instant, she melt like de lomp of sugar: she run to her bureau, and, in de minute, return wid de paper.

Sir *Geo.* Give it me. [*Reads.*

Les

Les preliminaires d'une traite entre le chevalier Wealthy, and la Signora Diamenti.

A bagatelle, a trifle: fhe fhall have it.

Load. Hark'e, knight, what is all that there outlandifh ftuff?

Sir *Geo.* Read, read! The eloquence of angels, my dear baron!

Load. Slam me, but the man's mad! I don't underftand their Gibberifh—What is it in Englifh?

Sir *Geo.* The preliminaries of a fubfidy treaty, between Sir G. Wealthy, and Signora Florenza? that the faid Signora will refign the poffeffion of her perfon to the faid Sir George, on the payment of three hundred guineas monthly, for equipage, table, domeftics, drefs, dogs, and diamonds; her debts to be duly difcharged, and a note advanced of five hundred by way of entrance.

Load. Zounds, what a cormorant! She muft be devilifh handfome.

Sir *Geo.* I am told fo.

Load. Told fo! Why did you never fee her?

Sir *Geo.* No; and poffibly never may, but from my box at the opera.

Load. Hey-dey! Why what the devil—

Sir *Geo.* Ha, ha, you ftare, I don't wonder at it, This is an elegant refinement, unknown to the grofs voluptuaries of this part of the world. This is, Mr. Loader, what may be called a debt to your dignity: for an opera girl is as effential a piece of equipage for a man of fafhion, as his coach.

Load. The devil!

Sir *Geo.* 'Tis for the vulgar only to enjoy what they poffefs: the diftinction of ranks and conditions are, to have hounds, and never hunt; cooks, and dine at taverns; houfes, you never inhabit; miftreffes, you never enjoy——

Load. And debts, you never pay. Egad, I am not furpriz'd at it; if this be your trade, no wonder that you want money for neceffaries, when you give fuch a damn'd deal for nothing at all.

Enter SERVANT.

Serv. Mrs. Cole, to wait upon your honour.

Sir *Geo.* My dear baron, run, difpatch my affair, conclude my treaty, and thank her for the very reafonable conditions.

Sir *Will.* I fall.

Sir *Geo.* Mr. Loader, fhall I trouble you to introduce the lady? She is, I think, your acquaintance.

Load. Who, old Moll? Ay, ay, fhe's your market-woman. I wou'd not give fix-pence for your fignoras. One armful of good, wholefome Britifh beauty, is worth a fhip-
load

load of their trapſing, tawdry trollops. But hark'e, baron, how much for the table? Why ſhe muſt have a deviliſh large family, or a monſtrous ſtomach.

Sir *Will.* Ay, ay, dere, is her moder, la complaiſante to walk in de Park, and to go to de play; two broders, deux valets, dree Spaniſh lap-dogs, and de monkey.

Load. Strip me, if I wou'd ſet five ſhillings againſt the whole gang. May my partner renounce with the game in his hand, if I were you, knight, if I would not———
[*Ex.* Bar.

Sir *Geo.* But the lady waits. [*Ex.* Load.] A ſtrange fellow this! What a whimſical jargon he talks! Not an idea abſtracted from play! To ſay truth, I am ſincerely ſick of my acquaintance: But, however, I have the firſt people in the kingdom to keep me in countenance. Death and the dice level all diſtinctions.

Enter Mrs. COLE, *ſupported by* LOADER *and* DICK.

Mrs. *Cole.* Gently, gently, good Mr. Loader,

Load. Come along, old Moll. Why, you jade, you look as roſy this morning, I muſt have a ſmack at your muns. Here, taſte her, ſhe is as good as old hock to get you a ſtomach.

Mrs. Cole. Fye, Mr. Loader, I thought you had forgot me.

Load. I forgot you! I would as foon forget what is trumps.

Mrs. Cole. Softly, foftly, young man. There, there, mighty well. And how does your honour do? I han't feen your honour, I can't tell the—Oh! mercy on me, there's a twinge———

Sir Geo. What is the matter, Mrs. Cole?

Mrs. Cole. My old diforder, the rheumatife; I han't been able to get a wink of—Oh la! what, you have been in town thefe two days?

Sir Geo. Since Wednefday.

Mrs. Cole. And never once call'd upon old Cole. No, no, I am worn out, thrown by and forgotten, like a tatter'd garment, as Mr. Squintum fays. Oh, he is a dear man! But for him I had been a loft fheep; never known the comforts of the new birth; no,—There's your old friend, Kitty Carrot, at home ftill. —What, fhall we fee you this evening? I have kept the green room for you ever fince I heard you were in town.

Load. What, fhall we take a fnap at old Moll's. Hey, beldam, have you a good batch of Burgundy abroach?

Mrs. Cole. Bright as a ruby; and for flavour! You know the colonel—He and Jenny Cummins drank three flafks, hand to fift, laft night.

Load.

Load. What, and bilk thee of thy share?

Mrs. Cole. Ah, don't mention it, Mr. Loader. No, that's all over with me. The time has been, when I could have earn'd thirty shillings a day by my own drinking, and the next morning was neither sick nor sorry: But now, O laud, a thimbleful turns me topsy-turvy.

Load. Poor old girl!

Mrs. Cole. Ay, I have done with these idle vanities; my thoughts are fix'd upon a better place.—What, I suppose, Mr. Loader, you will be for your old friend the black-ey'd girl, from Rosemary-lane. Ha, ha! Well, 'tis a merry little tit. A thousand pities she's such a reprobate!——But she'll mend; her time is not come: all shall have their call, as Mr. Squintum says, sooner or later; regeneration is not the work of a day. No, no, no,——Oh!

Sir *Geo.* Not worse I hope.

Mrs. Cole. Rack, rack, gnaw, gnaw, never easy a-bed or up all's one. Pray honest friend, have you any clary, or mint-water in the house?

Dick. A case of French drams.

Mrs. Cole. Heaven defend me! I would not touch a dram for the world.

Sir *Geo.* They are but cordials, Mrs. Cole. —Fetch 'em, you blockhead. [*Ex. Dick.*]

Mrs. Cole. Ay, I am a going; a wasting and a wasting, Sir George. What will become of the houſe when I am gone, heaven knows———No.——When people are miſs'd, then they are mourned. Sixteen years have I liv'd in the Garden, comfortably and creditably; and, tho' I ſay it, could have got bail any hour of the day: Reputable tradeſmen, Sir George, neighbours, Mr. Loader knows; no knock-me-down doings in my houſe. A ſet of regular, ſedate, ſober cuſtomers. No rioters.—Sixteen did I ſay— Ay, eighteen years I have paid ſcot and lot in the pariſh of St. Paul's, and during the whole time, nobody have ſaid, Mrs. Cole, why do you ſo? Unleſs twice that I was before Sir Thomas De Val, and three times in the round-houſe.

Sir Geo. Nay, don't weep, Mrs. Cole.

Load. May I loſe deal, with an honour at bottom, if old Moll does not bring tears into my eyes.

Mrs. *Cole.* However, it is a comfort after all, to think one has paſt thro' the world with credit and character. Ay, a good name, as Mr. Squintum ſays, is better than a gallipot of ointment.

Enter Dick, *with a dram.*

Load. Come, haſte, Dick, haſte; ſorrow is dry. Here, Moll, ſhall I fill thee a bumper?

Mrs.

Mrs. *Cole.* Hold, hold, Mr. Loader! Heaven help you, I could as soon swallow the Thames. Only a sip, to keep the gout out of my stomach.

Load. Why then, here's to thee.—Levant me, but it is supernaculum—Speak when you have enough.

Mrs. *Cole.* I won't trouble you for the glass; my hands do so tremble and shake, I shall but spill the good creature.

Load. Well pull'd. But now to business. Pr'ythee, Moll, did not I see a tight young wench in a linen gown, knock at your door this morning?

Mrs. *Cole.* Ay; a young thing from the country.

Load. Could we not get a peep at her this evening?

Mr. *Cole.* Impossible! She is engag'd to Sir Timothy Totter. I have taken earnest for her these three months.

Load. Pho, what signifies such a fellow as that! Tip him an old trader, and give her to the knight.

Mrs. *Cole.* Tip him an old trader! Mercy on us, where do you expect to go when you die, Mr. Loader?

Load. Crop me, but this Squintum has turn'd her brains.

Sir *Geo.* Nay, Mr. Loader, I think the gentleman has wrought a most happy reformation.

Mrs.

Mrs. *Cole.* Oh, it was a wonderful work. There had I been toffing in a fea of fin, without rudder or compafs. And had not the good gentleman piloted me into the harbour of grace, I muft have ftruck againft the rocks of reprobation, and have been quite fwallow'd up in the whirlpool of defpair. He was the precious inftrument of my fpiritual fprinkling.—But however, Sir George, if your mind be fet upon a young country thing, to-morrow night I believe I can furnifh you.

Load. As how?

Mrs. *Cole.* I have advertis'd this morning, in the regifter-office, for fervants under feventeen: and ten to one but I light on fomething that will do.

Load. Pillory me, but it has a face.

Mrs. *Cole.* Truly, confiftently with my confcience, I wou'd do any thing for your honour.

Sir *Geo.* Right, Mrs. Cole, never lofe fight of that monitor. But pray how long has this heavenly change been wrought in you?

Mrs. *Cole,* Ever fince my laft vifitation of the gout. Upon my firft fit, feven years ago, I began to have my doubts, and my waverings; but I was loft in a labyrinth, and no body to fhew me the road. One time, I thought of dying a Roman, which is truly a comfortable communion enough for one of us: but it wou'd not do.

Sir *Geo.* Why not?

Mrs. *Cole.* I went one summer over to Boulogne to repent; and, wou'd you believe it, the bare-footed, bald-pate beggars would not give me absolution, without I quitted my business——Did you ever hear of such a set of scabby——Besides, I cou'd not bear their barbarity. Would you believe it, Mr. Loader, they lock up for their lives, in a nunnery, the prettiest, sweetest, tender young things!——Oh, six of them, for a season, wou'd finish my business here, and then I shou'd have nothing to do, but to think of hereafter.

Load. Brand me, what a country!

Sir *Geo.* Oh, scandalous!

Mrs. *Cole.* O no, it would not do. So, in my last illness, I was wish'd to Mr. Squintum, who stept in with his saving grace, got me with the new birth, and I became as you see, regenerate, and another creature.

Enter DICK.

Dick. Mr. Transfer, sir, has sent to know if your honour be at home.

Sir *Geo.* Mrs. Cole, I am mortify'd to part with you. But business, you know—

Mrs. *Cole.* True, sir George, Mr. Loader, your arm——Gently, oh, oh!

Sir *Geo.* Wou'd you take another thimbleful, Mrs. Cole?

Mrs.

THE MINOR.

Mrs. *Cole.* Not a drop——I shall see you this evening?

Sir *Geo.* Depend upon me.

Mrs. *Cole.* To-morrow I hope to suit you ——We are to have, at the tabernacle, an occasional hynm, with a thanksgiving sermon for my recovery. After which, I shall call at the register office, and see what goods my advertisement has brought in.

Sir *Geo.* Extremely obliged to you, Mrs. Cole.

Mrs. *Cole.* Or if that should not do, I have a tit bit at home, will suit your stomach. Never brush'd by a beard. Well, heaven bless you—Softly, have a care, Mr. Loader ——Richard, you may as well give me the bottle into the chair, for fear I should be taken ill on the road. Gently——so, so!

[*Exit Mrs.* Cole *and* Loader.]

Sir *Geo.* Dick, shew Mr. Transfer in.—— Ha, ha, what a hodge podge! How the jade has jumbled together the carnal and the spiritual; with what ease she reconciles her new birth to her old calling! ——No wonder these preachers have plenty of proselytes, whilst they have the address so comfortably to blend the hitherto jarring interests of the two worlds.

Enter LOADER.

Well, knight, I have hous'd her; but they want you within, sir.

Sir *Geo.* I'll go to them immediately.

A C T

ACT II.

Enter Dick, *introducing* Transfer.

Dick. MY mafter will come to you prefently.

Enter Sir George.

Sir *Geo.* Mr. Transfer, your fervant.

Tranf. Your honour's very humble. I thought to have found Mr. Loader here.

Sir *Geo.* He will return immediately. Well, Mr. Transfer——but take a chair—you have had a long walk. Mr Loader, I prefume, open'd to you the urgency of my bufinefs.

Tranf. Ay, ay, the general cry, money, money! I don't know, for my part, where all the money is flown to. Formerly a note, with a tolerable endorfement, was as current as cafh. If your uncle Richard now wou'd join in this fecurity———

Sir *Geo.* Impoffible.

Tranf. Ay, like enough. I wifh you were of age.

Sir

Sir *Geo.* So do I. But as that will be confider'd in the premium.———

Tranſ. True, true,——I fee you underſtand buſ'neſs——And what fum does your honour lack at preſent?

Sir *Geo.* Lack!——How much have you brought?

Tranſ. Who, I? Dear me! none.

Sir *Geo.* Zounds, none!

Tranſ. Lack-a-day, none to be had, I think. All the morning have I been upon the hunt. There, Ephraim Barebones' the tallow chandler, in Thames-ſtreet, us'd to be a never-failing chap; not a guinea to be got there. Then I totter'd away to Nebuchadnezzar Zebulon, in the Old Jewry, but it happen'd to be Saturday; and they never touch on the Sabbath, you know.

Sir *Geo.* Why what the devil can I do?

Tranſ. Good me, I did not know your honour had been ſo prefs'd.

Sir *Geo.* My honour preſt! Yes, my honour is not only preſt, but ruin'd, unleſs I can raiſe money to redeem it. That blockhead Loader, to depend upon this old doating———

Tranſ. Well, well, now I declare, I am quite ſorry to ſee your honour in ſuch a taking.

Sir *Geo.* Damn your ſorrow.

Tranſ. But come, don't be caſt down: Tho' money is not to be had, money's worth may, and that's the ſame thing.

Sir

Sir Geo. How, dear Transfer?

Tranf. Why I have, at my warehouſe in the city, ten caſks of whale-blubber, a large cargo of Dantzick dowlas, with a curious aſſortment of Birmingham hafts, and Whitney blankets for exportation.

Sir Geo. Hey!

Tranf. And ſtay, ſtay, then, again, at my country-houſe, the bottom of Gray's inn-Lane, there's a hundred tun of fine old hay; only damag'd a little laſt winter, for want of thatching; with forty load of flint ſtones.

Sir Geo. Well.

Tranf. Your honour may have all theſe for a reaſonable profit, and convert them into caſh.

Sir Geo. Blubber and blankets? Why, you old raſcal, do you banter me?

Tranf. Who I? O law, marry heaven forbid.

Sir Geo. Get out of my—you ſtuttering ſcoundrel.

Tranf. If your honour wou'd but hear me——

Sir Geo. Troop, I ſay, unleſs you have a mind to go a ſhorter way than you came. [*Ex.* Tr.] And yet there is ſomething ſo uncommonly ridiculous in his propoſal, that were my mind more at eaſe. [*Enter* Loader.] So, ſir, you have recommended me to a fine fellow.

Load. What's the matter?

Sir

Sir *Geo.* He can't supply me with a shilling; and wants, besides, to make me a dealer in dowlas.

Load. Ay, and a very good commodity too. People that are upon ways and means, must not be nice, knight. A pretty piece of work you have made here! Thrown up the cards, with the game in your hands.

Sir *Geo.* Why, pr'ythee, of what use would his——

Load. Use! of every use.—Procure you the spankers, my boy. I have a broker, that in a twinkling, shall take off your bargain.

Sir *Geo.* Indeed!

Load. Indeed! Ay, indeed. You sit down to hazard and not know the chances! I'll call him back.—Hollo, Transfer.—A pretty little, busy, bustling—You may travel miles, before you will meet with his match. If there is one pound in the city, he will get it. He creeps, like a ferret, into their bags, and makes the yellow boys bolt again.

Enter TRANSFER.

Come hither, little Transfer; what, man, our Minor was a little too hasty; he did not understand trap: knows nothing of the game, my dear.

Transf. What I said, was to serve Sir George; as he seem'd——

Load. I told him so; well, well, we will take thy commodities, were they as many more.

more. But try, pr'ythee if thou coud'ft not procure us fome of the ready, for prefent fpending.

Tranf. Let me confider.

Load. Ay, do, come: fhuffle thy brains; never fear the baronet. To let a lord of lands want fhiners; 'tis a fhame.

Tranf. I do recollect, in this quarter of the town, an old friend, that us'd to do things in this way.

Load. Who?

Tranf. Statute, the fcrivener.

Load. Slam we, but he has nick'd the chance.

Tranf. A hard man, mafter Loader!

Sir *Geo.* No matter.

Tranf. His demands are exorbitant.

Sir *Geo.* That is no fault of ours.

Load. Well faid, knight!

Tranf. But to fave time, I had better mention his terms.

Load. Unneceffary.

Tranf. Five per cent. legal intereft.

Sir *Geo* He fhall have it.

Tranf. Ten, the præmium.

Sir *Geo.* No more words.

Tranf. Then, as you are not of age, five more for enfuring your life.

Load. We will give it.

Tranf. As for what he will demand for the rifque——

Sir *Geo.* He fhall be fatisfy'd.

E *Tranf.*

Tranf. You pay the attorney.

Sir *Geo.* Amply, amply; Loader, difpatch him.

Load. There, there, little Transfer; now every thing is fettled. All terms fhall be comply'd with, reafonable or unreafonable. What, our principal is a man of honour. [*Exit* Tr.] Hey, my knight, this is doing bufinefs. This pinch is a fure card.

Re-enter TRANSFER.

Tranf. I had forgot one thing. I am not the principal; you pay the brokerage.

Load. Ay, ay; and a handfome prefent into the bargain, never fear.

Tranf. Enough, enough.

Load. Hark'e, Transfer, we'll take the Birmingham hafts and Whitney wares.

Tranf. They fhall be forthcoming.—— You would not have the hay, with the flints?

Load. Every pebble of 'em. The magiftrates of the Baronet's borough are infirm and gouty. He fhall deal them as new pavement. [*Ex.* Tr.] So that's fettled. I believe, knight, I can lend you a helping hand as to the laft article. I know fome traders that will truck: fellows with finery, Not commodities of fuch clumfey conveyance as old Transfer's.

Sir *Geo.* You are obliging.

Load.

THE MINOR.

Load. I'll do it; boy; and get you, into the bargain, a bony auctioneer, that shall dispose of 'em all in a crack. [*Exit.*

Enter DICK.

Dick. Your uncle, sir, has been waiting some time.

Sir Geo. He comes in a lucky hour. Shew him in. [*Ex.* Dick.] Now for a lecture. My situation sha'n't sink my spirits, however. Here comes the musty trader, running over with remonstrances. I must banter the cit.

Enter RICHARD WEALTHY.

R. Weal. So, Sir, what I suppose, this is a spice of your foreign breeding, to let your uncle kick his heels in your hall, whilst your presence chamber is crouded with pimps, bawds, and gamesters.

Sir Geo. Oh, a proof of my respect, dear nuncle. Would it have been decent now, nuncle, to have introduced you into such company?

R. Weal. Wonderfully considerate! Well, young man, and what do you think will be the end of all this? Here I have received by the last mail, a quire of your draughts from abroad. I see you are determin'd our neighbours should taste of your magnificence.

Sir Geo. Yes, I think I did some credit to my country.

E 2 *R. Weal.*

R. Weal. And how are all thefe to be paid?

Sir Geo. That I fubmit to you, dear nuncle.

R. Weal. From me!——Not a foufe to keep you from the counter.

Sir Geo. Why then let the fcoundrels ftay. It is their duty. I have other demands, debts of honour, which muft be difcharg'd.

R. Weal. Here's a diabolical diftinction! Here's a proftitution of words!—Honour! 'Sdeath, that a rafcal, who has pick'd your pocket, fhall have his crime gilded with the moft facred diftinction, and his plunder punctually paid, whilft the induftrious mechanic, who minifters to your very wants, fhall have his debt delay'd, and his demand treated as infolent.

Sir Geo. Oh! a truce to this thread-bare trumpery, dear nuncle.

R. Weal. I confefs my folly; but, make yourfelf eafy; you won't be troubled with many more of my vifits. I own I was weak enough to defign a fhort expoftulation with you; but as we in the city know the true value of time, I fhall take care not to fquander away any more of it upon you.

Sir Geo. A prudent refolution.

R. Weal. One commiffion, however, I can't difpenfe with myfelf from executing. ——It was agreed between your father and me;

me, that as he had but one son and I one daughter——

Sir Geo. Your gettings should be added to his estate; and my cousin Margery and I squat down together in the comfortable state of matrimony.

R. Weal. Puppy! Such was our intention. Now his last will claims this contract.

Sir Geo. Dispatch, dear nuncle.

R. Weal. Why then, in a word, fee me here demand the execution.

Sir Geo. What dy'e mean? For me to marry Margery?

R. Weal. I do.

Sir Geo. What, moi-me?

R. Weal. You, you——Your answer, ay or no?

Sir Geo. Why then concisely and briefly, without evasion, equivocation, or further circumlocution,——No.

R. Weal. I am glad of it.

Sir Geo. So am I.

R. Weal. But pray, if it wou'd not be too great a favour, what objections can you have to my daughter? Not that I want to remove 'em, but merely out of curiosity, What objections?

Sir Geo. None. I neither know her, have seen her, enquired after her, or ever intend it.

R. Weal. What, perhaps, I am the stumbling block?

Sir Geo. You have hit it.

E 3 *R. Weal.*

R. Weal. Ay, now we come to the point. Well, and pray——

Sir *Geo.* Why it is not so much a dislike to your person, tho' that is exceptionable enough, but your profession, dear nuncle, is an insuperable obstacle.

R. Weal. Good lack! And what harm has that done, pray?

Sir *Geo.* Done! So stain'd, polluted, and tainted the whole mass of your blood, thrown such a blot on your 'scutcheon, as ten regular successions can hardly efface.

R. Weal. The deuce!

Sir *Geo.* And cou'd you now, consistently with your duty as a faithful guardian, recommend my union with the daughter of a trader?

R. Weal. Why, indeed, I ask pardon; I am afraid I did not weigh the matter as maturely as I ought,

Sir *Geo.* Oh, a horrid, barbarous scheme!

R. Weal. But then I thought her having the honour to partake of the same flesh and blood with yourself, might prove in some measure, a kind of fuller's-earth, to scour out the dirty spots contracted by commerce.

Sir *Geo.* Impossible!

R. Weal. Besides, here it has been the practice even of peers.

Sir *Geo.* Don't mention the unnatural intercourse! Thank heav'n, Mr. Richard Wealthy, my education has been in another country,

country, where I have been too well inſtructed in the value of nobility, to think of intermixing it with the offspring of a Bourgois. Why, what apology cou'd I make to my children, for giving them ſuch a mother?

R. Weal. I did not think of that. Then I muſt deſpair, I am afraid.

Sir *Geo.* I can afford but little hopes. Tho', upon recollection——Is the Griſſette pretty?

R. Weal. A parent may be partial. She is thought ſo.

Sir *Geo.* Ah la joile petite Bourgoiſe! Poor girl, I ſincerely pity her. And I ſuppoſe, to procure her emerſion from the mercantile mud, no conſideration wou'd be ſpar'd.

R. Weal. Why, to be ſure, for ſuch an honour, one wou'd ſtrain a point.

Sir *Geo.* Why then, not totally to deſtroy your hopes, I do recollect an edict in favour of Brittany; that when a man of diſtinction engages in commerce, his nobility is ſuffer'd to ſleep.

R. Weal. Indeed!

Sir *Geo.* And upon his quitting the contagious connection, he is permitted to reſume his rank.

R. Weal. That's fortunate.

Sir *Geo.* So, nuncle Richard, if you will ſell out of the ſtocks, ſhut up your counting-houſe,

house, and quit St. Mary Axe for Grosvenor-square——

R. Weal. What then?

Sir *Geo.* Why, when your rank has had time to rouse itself, for I think your nobility, nuncle, has had a pretty long nap, if the girl's person is pleasing, and the purchase-money is adequate to the honour, I may in time be prevail'd upon to restore her to the right of her family.

R. Weal. Amazing condescension!

Sir *Geo.* Good-nature is my foible. But, upon my soul, I wou'd not have gone so far for any body else.

R. Weal. I can contain no longer. — Hear me, spendthrift, prodigal, do you know, that in ten days your whole revenue won't purchase you a feather to adorn your empty head?——

Sir *Geo.* Hey dey, what's the matter now?

R. Weal. And that you derive every acre of your boasted patrimony from your great uncle, a soap-boiler!

Sir *Geo.* Infamous aspersion!

R. Weal. It was his bags, the fruits of his honest industry, that preserv'd your lazy, beggarly nobility. His wealth repair'd your tottering hall, from the ruins of which, even the rats had run.

Sir *Geo.* Better our name had perish'd! Insupportable! soap-boiling, uncle!

R. Weal.

R. Weal. Traduce a trader in a country of commerce! It is treason, against the community; and, for your punishment, I wou'd have you restor'd to the sordid condition from whence we drew you, and like your predecessors, the Picts, stript, painted, and fed upon hips, haws and blackberries.

Sir Geo. A truce, dear haberdasher.

R. Weal. One pleasure I have, that to this goal you are upon the gallop; but have a care, the sword hangs but by a thread. When next we meet, know me for the master of your fate. [*Exit.*

Sir Geo. Insolent mechanic! But that his Bourgois blood wou'd have foil'd my sword—

Enter BARON *and* LOADER.

Sir Will. What is de matter?

Sir Geo. A fellow here, upon the credit of a little affinity, has dar'd to upbraid me with being sprung from a soap-boiler.

Sir Will. Vat, you from the boiler of soap!

Sir Geo. Me.

Sir Will. Aha, begar, dat is anoder ting —And harka you, mister monsieur, ha— how dare a you have d'affrontary—

Sir Geo. How!

Sir Will. De impertinence to sit down, play wid me?

Sir Geo. What is this?

Sir Will. A beggarly Bourgois vis-a-vis, a baron of twenty descents.

Load.

Load. But baron——

Sir *Will.* Bygar, I am almoſt aſham'd to win of ſuch a low, dirty—Give me my monies, and let me never ſee your face.

Load. Why, but baron, you miſtake this thing, I know the old buck this fellow prates about.

Sir *Will.* May be.

Load. Pigeon me, as true a gentleman as the grand ſignor. He was, indeed, a good-natur'd, obliging, friendly fellow; and being a great judge of ſoap, tar, and train-oil, he us'd to have it home to his houſe, and ſell it to his acquaintance for ready money, to ſerve them.

Sir *Will.* Was dat all?

Load. Upon my honour.

Sir *Will.* Oh, dat, dat is anoder ting. Bygar I was afraid he was negotiant.

Load. Nothing like it.

Enter DICK.

Dick. A gentleman to enquire for Mr. Loader.

Load. I come—A pretty ſon of a bitch, this baron! pimps for the man, picks his pocket, and then wants to kick him out of company, becauſe his uncle was an oilman.
[*Exit.*

Sir *Will.* I beg pardon, chevalier, I was miſtake.

THE MINOR. 59

Sir *Geo.* Oh, don't mention it; had the flam been fact, your behaviour was natural enough.

Enter LOADER.

Load. Mr. Smirk, the auctioneer.
Sir *Geo.* Shew him in, by all means.
[*Exit* Loader.
Sir *Will.* You have affairs.
Sir *Geo.* If you'll walk into the next room, they will be finished in five minutes.

Enter LOADER, *with* SHIFT *as* SMIRK.

Load. Here, master Smirk, this is the gentleman. Hark'e, knight, did I not tell you, old Moll was your mark? Here she has brought a pretty piece of man's meat already; as sweet as a nosegay, and as ripe as a cherry, you rogue. Dispatch him, mean time we'll manage the girl. [*Exit.*
Smirk. You are the principal.
Sir *Geo.* Even so. I have, Mr. Smirk, some things of a considerable value, which I want to dispose of immediately.
Smirk. You have?
Sir *Geo.* Could you assist me?
Smirk. Doubtless.
Sir *Geo.* But directly?
Smirk. We have an auction at twelve. I'll add your cargo to the catalogue.
Sir *Geo.* Can that be done?

Smirk.

Smirk. Every day's practice: it is for the credit of the sale. Last week, amongst the valuable effects of a gentleman, going abroad, I sold a choice collection of china, with a curious service of plate; though the real party was never master of above two Delf dishes, and a dozen of pewter, in all his life.

Sir *Geo.* Very artificial. But this must be conceal'd.

Smirk. Bury'd here. Oh, many an aigrette and solitaire have I sold, to discharge a lady's play-debt. But then we must know the parties; otherwise it might be knockt down to the husband himself. Ha, ha—— Hey ho!

Sir *Geo.* True. Upon my word, your profession requires parts.

Smirk. No body's more. Did you ever hear Sir George, what first brought me into the business?

Sir *Geo.* Never.

Smirk. Quite an accident, as I may say. You must have known my predecessor, Mr. Prig, the greatest man in the world, in his way, ay, or that ever was, or ever will be; quite a jewel of a man: he would touch you up a lot; there was no resisting him. He wou'd force you to bid, whether you wou'd or no. I shall never see his equal.

Sir *Geo.* You are modest, Mr. Smirk.

Smirk.

Smirk. No, no, but his shadow. Far be it from me, to vie with so great a man. But as I was saying, my predeceſſor, Mr. Prig, was to have a ſale as it might be on a Saturday. On Friday at noon, I shall never forget the day, he was ſuddenly ſeized with a violent cholic. He ſent for me to his bed-ſide, ſqueez'd me by the hand; Dear Smirk, ſaid he, what an accident? You know what is to-morrow; the greateſt ſhew this ſeaſon;—prints, pictures, bronzes, butterflies, medals, and minionettes; all the world will be there; lady Dy Jos, Mrs. Nankyn, the dutcheſs of Dupe, and every body at all; You ſee my ſtate, it will be impoſſible for me to mount. What can I do?—It was not for me, you know, to adviſe that great man.

Sir *Geo.* No, no.

Smirk. At laſt, looking wiſhfully at me, Smirk, ſays he, d'you love me?—Mr. Prig, can you doubt it?——I'll put it to the teſt, ſays he; ſupply my place to-morrow.— I, eager to ſhew my love, raſhly and rapidly replied I will.

Sir. *Geo.* That was bold.

Smirk. Abſolute madneſs. But I had gone too far to recede. Then the point was, to prepare for the awful occaſion. The firſt want that occurred to me, was a wig; but this was too material an article to depend on my own judgment. I reſolved to conſult my friends. I told them the affair——You

hear,

hear, gentlemen, what has happen'd; Mr. Prig, one of the greatest men in his way, the world ever saw, or ever will, quite a jewel of a man, taken with a violent fit of the cholic; to-morrow, the greatest shew this season; prints, pictures, bronzes, butterflies, medals, and minionettes; every body in the world to be there; lady Dy Joss, Mrs. Nankyn, dutchess of Dupe, and all mankind; it being impossible he should mount, I have consented to fell——They star'd—It is true, gentlemen. Now I should be glad to have your opinions as to a wig. They were divided: some recommended a tye, others a bag: one mention'd a bob, but was soon over-rul'd. Now, for my part, I own, I rather inclin'd to the bag; but to avoid the imputation of rashness, I resolv'd to take Mrs. Smirk's judgment, my wife, a dear good woman, fine in figure, high in taste, a superior genius, and knows old china like a Nabob.

Sir Geo. What was her decision?

Smirk. I told her the case—My dear, you know what has happen'd. My good friend, Mr. Prig, the greatest man in the world, in his way, that ever was, or ever will be, quite a jewel of a man—a violent fit of the cholic ——the greatest shew this season, to-morrow, pictures, and every thing in the world; all the world will be there: now, as it is impossible he should, I mount in his stead.

You

You know the importance of a wig; I have aſk'd my friends—ſome recommended a tye, others a bag—what is your opinion? Why, to deal freely, Mr. Smirk, ſays ſhe, a tye for your round, regular, ſmiling face would be rather too formal, and a bag too boyiſh, deficient in dignity for the ſolemn occaſion; were I worthy to adviſe, you ſhould wear a ſomething between both.—I'll be hang'd, if you don't mean a major. I jumpt at the hint, and a major it was.

Sir *Geo.* So, that was fixt.

Smirk. Finally. But next day, when I came to mount the roſtrum, then was the trial. My limbs ſhook, and my tongue trembled. The firſt lot was a chamber-utenſil, in Chelſea china, of the pea-green pattern. It occaſioned a great laugh; but I got thro' it. Her grace indeed, gave me great encouragement. I overheard her whiſper to lady Dy, Upon my word, Mr. Smirk does it very well. Very well, indeed, Mr. Smirk, addreſſing herſelf to me. I made an acknowledging bow to her grace, as in duty bound. But one flower flounced involuntarily from me that day, as I may ſay. I remember, Dr. Trifle call'd it enthuſiaſtic, and pronounc'd it a preſage of my future greatneſs.

Sir *Geo.* What was that?

Smirk. Why, ſir, the lot was a Guido; a ſingle figure, a marvellous fine performance;
well

well preferv'd, and highly finifh'd. It ftuck at five and forty; I, charm'd with the picture, and piqu'd at the people, A going for five and forty, no body more than five and forty?——Pray, ladies and gentlemen, look at this piece, quite flefh and blood, and only wants a touch from the torch of Prometheus, to ftart from the canvas and fall a bidding. A general plaudit enfu'd, I bow'd, and in three minutes knock'd it down at fixty three, ten.

Sir Geo. That was a ftroke at leaft equal to your mafter.

Snurk. O dear me! You did not know the great man, alike in every thing. He had as much to fay upon a ribbon as a Raphael. His manner was inimitably fine. I remember, they took him off at the playhoufe, fome time ago; pleafant, but wrong. Public characters fhou'd not be fported with ——They are facred——But we lofe time.

Sir Geo. Oh, in the lobby, on the table, you will find the particulars.

Smirk. We fhall fee you. There will be a world of company. I fhall pleafe you. But the great nicety of our art is, the eye. Mark how mine fkims round the room. Some bidders are fhy, and only advance with a nod; but I nail them. One, two, three, four, five. You will be furpriz'd—Ha, ha, ha,—heigh ho! [*Exit.*

ACT

Enter Sir GEORGE *and* LOADER.

Sir *George.*

A Most infernal run. Let's see, *(Pulls out a card.)* Loader a thousand, the Baron two, Tally——Enough to beggar a banker. Every shilling of Transfer's supply exhausted! nor will even the sale of my moveables prove sufficient to discharge my debts. Death and the devil! In what a complication of calamities has a few days plung'd me! And no resource?

Load. Knight, here's old Moll come to wait on you; she has brought the tid-bit I spoke of. Shall I bid her send her in?

Sir *Geo.* Pray do. [*Exit* Loader.

Enter Mrs. COLE *and* LUCY.

Mrs. *Cole.* Come along, Lucy. You bashful baggage, I thought I had silenc'd your scruples. Don't you remember what Mr. Squintum said? A woman's not worth saving, that won't be guilty of a swinging sin; for then they have matter to repent upon. Here your honour, I leave her to your management.

nagement. She is young, tender, and timid; does not know what is for her own good; but your honour will soon teach her. I wou'd willingly stay, but I must not lose the lecture. [*Exit.*

Sir *Geo.* Upon my credit, a fine figure! Aukward——Can't produce her publicly as mine; but she will do for private amusement ——Will you be seated, miss?——Dumb! quite a picture! She too wants a touch of the Promethean torch—Will you be so kind, ma'am, to walk from your frame and take a chair?——Come, pr'ythee, why so coy? Nay, I am not very adroit in the custom of this country. I suppose I must conduct you ——Come, miss.

Lucy. O, sir.

Sir *Geo.* Child!

Lucy. If you have any humanity, spare me.

Sir *Geo.* In tears! What can this mean? Artifice. A project to raise the price, I suppose. Look'e, my dear, you may save this piece of pathetic for another occasion. It won't do with me; I am no novice—— So, child, a truce to your tragedy, I beg.

Lucy. Indeed you wrong me, sir; indeed you do.

Sir *Geo.* Wrong you! how came you here, and for what purpose?

Lucy.

Lucy. A shameful one, I know it all, and yet believe me, sir, I am innocent.

Sir Geo. Oh, I don't question that. Your pious patroness is a proof of your innocence.

Lucy. What can I say to gain your credit? And yet, sir, strong as appearances are against me, by all that's holy, you see me here, a poor distrest, involuntary victim.

Sir Geo. Her style's above the common class; her tears are real.—Rise, child.—How the poor creature trembles!

Lucy. Say then I am safe.

Sir Geo. Fear nothing.

Lucy. May heaven reward you. I cannot.

Sir Geo. Pr'ythee, child, collect yourself, and help me to unravel this mystery. You came hither willingly? There was no force?

Lucy. None.

Sir Geo. You know Mrs. Cole.

Lucy. Too well.

Sir Geo. How came you then to trust her?

Lucy. Mine, sir, is a tedious, melancholy tale.

Sir Geo. And artless too?

Lucy. As innocence.

Sir Geo. Give it me.

Lucy. It will tire you.

Sir Geo. Not if it be true. Be just, and you will find me generous.

Lucy: On that, fir, I rely'd in venturing hither.

Sir Geo. You did me juftice. Truft me with all your ftory. If you deferve, depend upon my protection.

Lucy: Some months ago, fir, I was confider'd as the joint heirefs of a refpectable, wealthy merchant; dear to my friends, happy in my profpects, and my father's favourite.

Sir *Geo.* His name

Lucy. There you muft pardon me. Unkind and cruel tho' he has been to me, let me difcharge the duty of a daughter, fuffer in filence, nor bring reproach on him who gave me being.

Sir *Geo.* I applaud your piety.

Lucy. At this happy period, my father, judging an addition of wealth muft bring an increafe of happinefs, refolved to unite me with a man, fordid in his mind, brutal in his manners, and riches his only recommendation. My refufal of this ill-fuited match, tho' mildly given, enflamed my father's temper, naturally choleric, alienated his affections, and banifh'd me his houfe, diftreft and deftitute.

Sir *Geo.* Wou'd no friend receive you?

Lucy. Alas, how few are friends to the unfortunate! Befides, I knew, fir, fuch a ftep wou'd be confider'd by my father, as an

appeal

appeal from his juſtice. I, therefore, retir'd to a remote corner of the town, truſting, as my only advocate, to the tender calls of nature, in his cool, reflecting hours.

Sir *Geo.* How came you to know this woman?

Lucy. Accident plac'd me in a houſe, the miſtreſs of which profeſs'd the ſame principles with my infamous conductreſs. There, as enthuſiaſm is the child of melancholy, I caught the infection. A conſtant attendance on their aſſemblies procured me the acquaintance of this woman, whoſe extraordinary zeal and devotion firſt drew my attention and confidence. I truſted her with my ſtory, and in return, receiv'd the warmeſt invitation to take the protection of her houſe. This I unfortunately accepted.

Sir *Geo.* Unfortunately indeed!

Lucy. By the decency of appearances, I was ſome time impoſed upon. But an accident, which you will excuſe my repeating, reveal'd all the horror of my ſituation. I will not trouble you with a recital of all the arts us'd to ſeduce me: Happily they hitherto have fail'd. But this morning I was acquainted with my deſtiny; and no other election left me, but immediate compliance, or a jail. In this deſperate condition, you cannot wonder, ſir, at my chooſing rather to rely on the generoſity of a gentleman, than

F 3 the

the humanity of a creature infenfible to pity, and void of every virtue.

Sir Geo. The event fhall juftify your choice. You have my faith and honour for your fecurity. For tho' I can't boaft of my own goodnefs, yet I have an honeft feeling for afflicted virtue; and, however unfafhionable, a fpirit that dares afford it protection. Give me your hand. As foon as I have difpatch'd fome preffing bufinefs here, I will lodge you in an afylum, facred to the diftreffes of your fex; where indigent beauty is guarded from temptations, and deluded innocence refcu'd from infamy.

[*Exeunt.*

Enter SHIFT.

Zooks, I have toil'd like a horfe; quite tir'd, by Jupiter. And what fhall I get for my pains? The old fellow here talks of making me eafy for life. Eafy! And what does he mean by eafy? He'll make me an excife-man, I fuppofe, and fo with an inkhorn at my button-hole, and a taper fwitch in my hand, I fhall run about gauging of beer-barrels. No, that will never do. This lad here is no fool. Foppifh indeed. He does not want parts, no, nor principles neither. I overheard his fcene with the girl. I think I may truft him. I have a great mind to venture it. It is a fhame to have him

dup'd

dup'd by this old don. It muſt not be, I'll in and unfold—Ha!—Egad, I have a thought too which, if my heir apparent can execute, I ſhall ſtill lie conceal'd, and perhaps be rewarded on both ſides.

I have it,—'tis engender'd, piping hot,
And now, Sir Knight, I'll match you with
  a plot. [*Exit.*

Enter Sir WILLIAM *and* RICHARD WEALTHY.

R. Weal. Well, I ſuppoſe, by this time, you are ſatisfied what a ſcoundrel you have brought into the world, and are ready to finiſh your foolery.

Sir *Will.* Got to the cataſtrophe, good brother.

R. Weal. Let us have it over then.

Sir *Will.* I have already alarmed all his tradeſmen. I ſuppoſe we ſhall ſoon have him here, with a legion of bailiffs and conſtables.——Oh, you have my will about you?

R. Weal. Yes, yes.

Sir *Will.* It is almoſt time to produce it, or read him the clauſe that relates to his rejecting your daughter. That will do his buſineſs. But they come. I muſt return to my character.

Enter

Enter SHIFT.

Shift. Sir, sir, we are all in the wrong box; our scheme is blown up; your son has detected Loader and Tally, and is playing the very devil within.
Sir Will. Oh, the bunglers!
Shift. Now for it, youngster.

Enter Sir GEORGE, *driving in* LOADER *and another.*

Sir Geo. Rascals, robbers, that, like the locust, mark the road you have taken, by the ruin and desolation you leave behind you.
Load. Sir George!
Sir Geo. And can youth, however cautious, be guarded against such deep-laid, complicated villainy? Where are the rest of your diabolical crew? your auctioneer, usurer, and——O sir, are you here?——I am glad you have not escaped us, however.
Sir Will. What de devil is de matter?
Sir Geo. Your birth, which I believe an imposition, preserves you, however, from the discipline those rogues have receiv'd. A baron, a nobleman, a sharper! O shame! It is enough to banish all confidence, from the world. On whose faith can we rely, when those,

those, whose honour is held as sacred as an oath, unmindful of their dignity, descend to rival pick-pockets in their infamous arts. What are these [*pulls out dice*] pretty implements? The fruits of your leisure hours! They are dexterously done. You have a fine mechanical turn.—Dick, secure the door.

Mrs. Cole, *speaking as entering.*

Mrs. *Cole.* Here I am, at last. Well, and how is your honour, and the little gentlewoman?—Bless me! what is the matter here?

Sir *Geo.* I am, madam, treating your friends with a cold collation, and you are opportunely come for your share. The little gentlewoman is safe, and in much better hands than you designed her. Abominable hypocrite! who, tottering under the load of irrevent age and infamous diseases, inflexibly proceed in the practice of every vice, impiously prostituting the most sacred institutions to the most infernal purposes.

Mrs. *Cole.* I hope your honour.——

Sir *Geo.* Take her away, As you have been singular in your penitence, you ought to be distinguish'd in your penance; which I promise you, shall be most publickly and plentifully bestow'd. [*Exit* Cole.

Enter

Enter Dick.

Dick. The conſtables, ſir.

Sir *Geo.* Let them come in, that I may conſign theſe gentlemen to their care. [*To Sir* Will.] Your letters of nobility you will produce in a court of juſtice. Tho', if I read you right, you are one of thoſe indigent, itinerant nobles of your own creation, which our reputation for hoſpitality draws hither in ſhoals, to the ſhame of our underſtanding, the imparing of our fortunes, and when you are truſted, the betraying of our deſigns. Officers, do your duty.

Sir *Will.* Why, don't you know me?

Sir *Geo.* Juſt as I gueſs'd. An impoſtor. He has recover'd the free uſe of his tongue already.

Sir *Will.* Nay, but George.

Sir *Geo.* Inſolent familiarity! away with him.

Sir *Will.* Hold, hold, a moment. Brother Richard, ſet this matter to rights.

R. Weal. Don't you know him?

Sir *Geo.* Know him! The very queſtion is an affront.

R. Weal. Nay, I don't wonder at it. 'Tis your father, you fool.

Sir *Geo.* My father! Impoſſible!

Sir *Will.* That may be, but 'tis true.

Sir

Sir *Geo.* My father alive? Thus let me greet the blessing.

Sir *Will.* Alive! Ay, and I believe I shan't be in a hurry to die again.

Sir *Geo.* But, dear sir, the report of your death——and this disg..se——to what——.

Sir *Will.* Don't ask any questions. Your uncle will tell you all. For my part, I am sick of the scheme.

R. Weal. I told you what would come of your politicks.

Sir *Will.* You did so. But if it had not been for those clumsy scoundrels, the plot was as good a plot.——O George, such discoveries I have to make. Within I'll unravel the whole.

Sir *Geo.* Perhaps, sir, I may match 'em.

Shift. Sir. [*Pulls him by the sleeve.*

Sir *Geo.* Never fear. It is impossible, gentlemen, to determine your fate, till this matter is more fully explain'd; till when, keep 'em in safe custody.——Do you know them, sir?

Sir *Will.* Yes, but that's more than they did me. I can cancel your debts there, and, I believe prevail on those gentlemen to refund too——But you have been a sad profligate young dog, George.

Sir *Geo.* I can't boast of my goodness, sir, but I think I could produce you a proof, that I am not so totally destitute of——

Sir

Sir *Wil.* Ay! Why then pr'ythee do.

Sir *Geo.* I have, sir, this day, resisted a temptation, that greater pretenders to morality might have yielded to. But I will trust myself no longer, and must crave your interposition and protection.

Sir *Will.* To what?

Sir *Geo.* I will attend you with the explanation in an instant. [*Exit.*

Sir *Will.* Pr'ythee, Shift, what does he mean?

Shift. I believe I can guess.

Sir *Will.* Let us have it.

Shift. I suppose the affair I overheard just now, a prodigious fine elegant girl, faith, that, discarded by her family, for refusing to marry her grandfather, fell into the hands of the venerable lady you saw, who being the kind caterer for your son's amusements, brought her hither for a purpose obvious enough. But the young gentleman, touch'd with her story, truth, and tears, was converted from the spoiler of her honour to the protector of her innocence.

Sir *Will.* Look'e there, brother, did not I tell you that George was not so bad at the bottom!

R. Weal. This does indeed atone for half the——But they are here.

Enter

Enter Sir GEORGE *and* LUCY.

Sir Geo. Fear nothing, madam, you may safely rely on the——
Lucy. My father!
R. Weal. Lucy!
Lucy. O, fir, can you forgive your poor diftreft unhappy girl? You fcarce can guefs how hardly I've been us'd, fince my banifhment from your paternal roof. Want, pining want, anguifh and fhame, have been my conftant partners.
Sir Will. Brother!
Sir Geo. Sir!
Lucy. Father!
R. Weal. Rife, child, 'tis I muft afk thee forgivenefs. Canft thou forget the woes I've made thee fuffer? Come to my arms once more, thou darling of my age.—What mifchief had my rafhnefs nearly compleated. Nephew, I fcarce can thank you as I ought, but——
Sir Geo. I am richly paid, in being the happy inftrument——Yet, might I urge a wifh——
R. Weal. Name it.
Sir Geo. That you would forgive my follies of to-day; and, as I have been providentially the occafional guardian of your

daughter's

daughter's honour, that you would bestow on me that right for life.

R. Weal. That must depend on Lucy; her will, not mine, shall now direct her choice—What says your father?

Sir *Will.* Me! Oh, I'll shew you in an instant. Give me your hands. There children, now you are join'd, and the devil take him that wishes to part you.

Sir *Geo.* I thank you for us both.

R. Weal. Happiness attend you.

Sir *Will.* Now, brother, I hope you will allow me to be a good plotter. All this was brought to bear by my means.

Shift. With my assistance, I hope you'll own, sir.

Sir *Will.* That's true, honest Shift, and thou shalt be richly rewarded; nay, George shall be your friend too. This Shift is an ingenious fellow, let me tell you, son.

Sir *Geo.* I am no stranger to his abilities, sir. But, if you please, we will retire. The various struggles of this fair sufferer require the soothing softness of a sister's love. And now, sir, I hope your fears for me are over; for had I not this motive to restrain my follies, yet I now know the town too well to be ever its bubble, and will take care to preserve, at least,

Some more estate, and principles, and wit,
Than brokers, bawds, and gamesters shall think fit.

S H I F T,

SHIFT, *addreſſing himſelf to Sir* George.

And what becomes of your poor fervant Shift?
Your father talks of lending me a lift———
A great man's promiſe, when his turn is ferv'd!
Capons on promiſes wou'd foon be ſtarv'd:
No, on myſelf alone, I'll now rely:
'Gad I've a thriving traffic in my eye———
Near the mad manſions of Moorfields I'll bawl;
Friends, fathers, mothers, fiſters, fons, and all,
Shut up your ſhops, and liſten to my call.
With labour, toil, all ſecond means diſpenſe,
And live a rent-charge upon Providence.
Prick up your ears; a ſtory now I'll tell,
Which once a widow, and her child befel,
I knew the mother, and her daughter well;
Poor, it is true, they were; but never wanted,
For whatſoe'er they aſk'd, was always granted:
One fatal day, the matron's truth was try'd,
She wanted meat and drink, and fairly cry'd.
[*Child.*] Mother, you cry! [*Moth.*] Oh, child,
    I've got no bread.
[*Child.*] What matter that? Why Providence an't
    dead!
With reaſon good, this truth the child might ſay,
For there came in at noon, that very day,
Bread, greens, potatoes, and a leg of mutton,
A better ſure a table ne'er was put on:
Ay, that might be, ye cry, with thoſe poor ſouls;
But we ne'er had a raſher for the coals.
And d'ye deſerve it? How d'ye ſpend your days?
In paſtimes, prodigality, and plays!
Let's go ſee Foote? ah, Foote's a precious limb!
Old-nick will foon a football make of him!

For

For foremoſt rows in ſide-boxes you ſhove,
Think you to meet with ſide-boxes above?
Where gigling girls and powder'd fops may ſit,
No, you will all be cramm'd into the pit,
And croud the houſe for Satan's benefit.
Oh, what you ſnivel? well, do ſo no more,
Drop, to atone, your money at the door,
And, if I pleaſe,——I'll give it to the poor.

FINIS.

THE

LYAR.

A

COMEDY

IN THREE ACTS,

As it is Performed at the

THEATRE in the HAY-MARKET.

BY SAMUEL FOOTE, ESQ.

———

LONDON:
Printed for W. LOWNDES, J. RIVINGTON and SONS,
And S. BLADON, in PATER-NOSTER-ROW,
M DCCLXXXVI.
[Price One Shilling and Six-pence.]

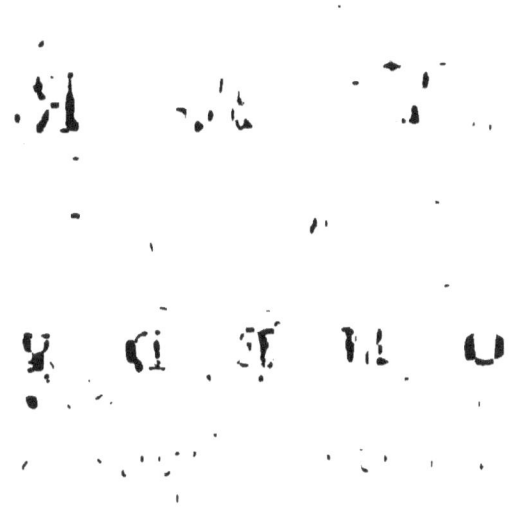

PROLOGUE.

*W*HAT various revolutions in our art,
    Since Thespis first sung ballads in a cart!
By nature fram'd the witty war to wage,
And lay the deep foundations of the stage,
From his own soil that bard his pictures drew:
The gaping crowd the mimic features knew,
And the broad jest with fire electric flew.
Succeeding times, more polish'd and refin'd.
To rigid rules the comic muse confin'd:
Robb'd of the nat'ral freedom of her song,
In artful measures now she floats along;
No sprightly sallies rouse the slumb'ring pit;
Thalia, grown mere architect in wit,
To doors and ladders has confin'd her cares,
Convenient closets, and a snug back stairs;
'Twixt her and Satire has dissolv'd the league,
And jilted humour to enjoy intrigue.
To gain the suffrage of this polish'd age,
We bring to-night a stranger on the stage:
His sire De Vega; we confess this truth,
Lest you mistake him for a British youth.
Severe the censure on my feeble pen,
Neglecting manners, that she copies men:
Thus, if I hum or ha, or name report,
'Tis Serjeant Splitcause from the Inns of Court;
If, at the age that ladies cease to dance,
To romp at Ranelagh, or read romance,
I draw a dowager inclin'd to man,
Or paint her rage for china or japan,
The true original is quickly known,
And lady Squab proclaim'd throughout the town.
But in the following group let no man dare
To claim a limb, nay, not a single hair:
What gallant Briton can be such a sot
To own the child a Spaniard has begot.

Dramatis Personæ.

Sir JAMES ELLIOT,   Mr. *R. Palmer.*
OLD WILDING, the Father, Mr. *Fearon.*
YOUNG WILDING,   Mr. *Palmer.*
PAPILLION,   Mr. *Baddeley.*

Miss GRANTAM,   Mrs. *Hitchcock.*
Miss GODFREY,   Miss *Platt.*
KITTY, the Maid,   Mrs. *Poussin.*

The Servants.

THE
LYAR.

ACT I.

Scene a Lodging.

Young Wilding and Papillion *discovered*.

Young Wilding.

AND I am now, Papillion, perfectly equipped?

Papillion. Perſonne mieux. Nobody better.

Y. Wild. My figure?

Pap. Fait a peindre.

Y. Wild. My air?

Pap. Libre.

Y. Wild. My addreſs?

Pap. Pariſiene.

Y. Wild. My hat fits eaſily under my arm; not like the draggled tail of my tatter'd academical habit.

Pap. Ah, bein autre choſe.

Y. Wild. Why then adieu, Alma Mater, and bien venue, la ville de Londre; farewell to the ſchools, and welcome the theatres; preſidents, proctors, ſhort commons with long graces, muſt now give place to plays, bagnios, long tavern-bills with no graces at all.

Pap.

Pap. Ah, bravo, bravo !

Y. Wild. Well, but my dear Papillion, you muſt give me the chart du paye: This town is a new world to me; my provident papa, you know would never ſuffer me near the ſmoak of London; and what can be his motive for permitting me now, I can't readily conceive.

Pap. Ni moi.

Y. Wild. I ſhall, however, take the liberty to conceal my arrival from him for a few days.

Pap. Vous avez raiſon.

Y. Wild. Well, my Mentor, and how am I to manage? direct my road: where muſt I begin? But the debate is, I ſuppoſe, of conſequence?

Pap. Vraiment.

Y. Wild. How long have you left Paris, Papillion?

Pap. Twelve, dirteen year.

Y. Wild. I can't compliment you upon your progreſs in Engliſh.

Pap. The accent is difficult.

Y. Wild. But here you are at home.

Pap. C'eſt vrai.

Y. Wild. No ſtranger to faſhionable places.

Pap. O faite!

Y. Wild. Acquainted with the faſhionable figure of both ſexes.

Pap. Sans doute.

Y. Wild. Well then, upon your lecture: And, d'ye hear, Papillion, as you have the honour to be promoted from the mortifying condition of an humble valet, to the important charge of a private tutor, let us diſcard all diſtance between us: See me ready to ſlack my thirſt at your fountain of knowledge, my Magnus Apollo.

Pap. Here then I diſcloſe my Helicon to my poetical pupil.

Y. Wild.

Y. Wild. Hey, Papillion!
Pap. Sir?
Y. Wild. What is this? why you speak English!
Pap. Without doubt.
Y. Wild. But like a native;
Pap. To be sure.
Y. Wild. And what am I to conclude from all this?
Pap. Logically thus, Sir: Whoever speaks pure English is an Englishman; I speak pure English; ergo, I am an Englishman. There's a categorical syllogism for you, Major, Minor, and Consequence. What do you think, Sir, that whilst you was busy at Oxford, I was idle? no, no, no.
Y. Wild. Well, Sir, but notwithstanding your pleasantry, I must have this matter explain'd.
Pap. So you shall, my good Sir; but don't be in such a hurry: You can't suppose I would give you the key, unless I meant you should open the door.
Y. Wild. Why then. prithee unlock.
Pap. Immediately. But by way of entering upon my post as preceptor, suffer me first to give you a hint: You must not expect, Sir, to find here, as at Oxford, men appearing in their real characters; every body there, Sir, knows that Dr. Muffy is a fellow of Maudlin, and Tom Trifle a student of Christchurch; but this town is one great comedy, in which not only the principles, but frequently the persons are feigned.
Y. Wild. A useful observation.
Pap. Why now, Sir, at the first coffee-house I shall enter you, you will perhaps meet a man from whose decent sable dress, placid countenance, insinuating behaviour, short sword, with the waiter's civil addition of " a dish of coffee
for

for Dr. Julap," you would suppose him to be a physician.

Y. Wild. Well?

Pap. Does not know diascordium from diaculum. An absolute French spy, concealed under the shelter of a huge medicinal perriwig.

Y. Wild. Indeed!

Pap. A martial figure too, it is odds but you will encounter; from whose scars, title, dress, and address, you would suppose to have had a share in every action since the peace of the Pyrenees; runner to a gaming-table, and bully to a bawdy-house. Battles to be sure he has been in—with the watch; and frequently a prisoner too—in the round-house.

Y. Wild. Amazing!

Pap. In short, Sir, you will meet with lawyers who practise smuggling, and merchants who trade upon Hounslow-heath; reverend atheists, right honourable sharpers, and Frenchmen from the county of York.

Y. Wild. In the last list, I presume, you roll.

Pap. Just my situation.

Y. Wild. And pray, Sir, what may be your motive for this whimsical transformation?

Pap. A very harmless one, I promise you: I would only avail myself at the expence of folly and prejudice.

Y. Wild. As how?

Pap. Why, Sir——But, to be better understood, I believe it will be necessary to give you a short sketch of the principal incidents of my life.

Y. Wild. Prithee do.

Pap. Why then you are to know, Sir, that my former situation has been rather above my present condition, having once sustained the dignity of sub-preceptor to one of those cheap rural
academies

academies with which our county of York is so plentifully stocked.

Y. Wild. But to the point: Why this disguise? Why renounce your country?

Pap. There, Sir, you make a little mistake; it was my country that renounced me.

Y. Wild. Explain.

Pap. In an instant; upon quitting the school, and first coming to town, I got recommended to the compiler of the Monthly Review.

Y. Wild. What an author too?

Pap. Oh, a voluminous one: the whole region of the belles lettres fell under my inspection; physic, divinity, and the mathematics, my mistress managed herself. There, Sir, like another Aristarch, I dealt out fame and damnation at pleasure. In obedience to the caprice and commands of my master, I have condemn'd books I never read, and applauded the fidelity of a translation, without understanding one syllable of the original.

Y. Wild. Ah! why I thought acuteness of discernment, and depth of knowledge, were necessary to accomplish a critic.

Pap. Yes, Sir; but not a monthly one. Our method was very concise: We copy the title-page of a new book; we never go any further: If we are ordered to praise it, we have at hand about ten words, which, scatter'd through as many periods, effectually does the business; as, " laudable design, happy arrangement, spirited language, nervous sentiment, elevation of thought, conclusive argument;" if we are to decry, then we have, " unconnected, flat, false, illiberal stricture, reprehensible, unnatural:" And thus, Sir, we pepper the author, and soon rid our hands of his work.

Y. Wild.

Y. Wild. A short recipe.

Pap. And yet, Sir, you have all the materials that are necessary: These are the arms with which we engage authors of every kind. To us all subjects are equal; plays or sermons, poetry or politics, music or midwifry, it is the same thing.

Y. Wild. How came you to resign this easy employment?

Pap. It would not answer. Notwithstanding what we say, people will judge for themselves; our work hung upon hand, and all I could get from the publisher was four shillings a-week, and my small beer. Poor pittance!

Y. Wild. Poor indeed.

Pap. Oh, half starv'd me!

Y. Wild. What was your next change?

Pap. I was mightily puzzled to choose. Some would have had me turn player, and others methodist preacher; but as I had no money to build me a tabernacle, I did not think it could answer; and as to player—whatever might happen to me, I was determined not to bring a disgrace upon my family, and so I resolved to turn footman.

Y. Wild. Wisely resolv'd.

Pap. Yes, Sir, but not so easily executed.

Y. Wild. No!

Pap. Oh no, Sir. Many a weary step have I taken after a place: Here I was too old, there I was too young; here the last livery was too big, there it was too little; here I was awkard, there I was knowing; madam dislik'd me at this house, her ladyship's woman at the next; so that I was as much puzzled to find out a place, as the great Cynic philosopher to discover a man. In short, I was quite in a state of despair, when chance threw an old friend in my way that quite retrieved my affairs. *Y. Wild.*

Y. Wild. Pray who might he be?

Pap. A little bit of a Swifs genius, who had been French ufher with me at the fame fchool in the country. I opened my melancholy ftory to him over three-pennyworth of beef-a-la-mode, in a cellar in St. Ann's. My little foreign friend purs'd up his lanthorn jaws, and with a fhrug of contempt, " Ah, maitre Jean, vous n'avez pas la politique; you have no fineffe: To trive here you muft ftudy the folly of your own country." " How, Monfieur!" " 'Taifez vous. Keep a your tongue! autre foy! I teach you fpeak French, now I teach a you to forget Englifh. Go vid me to my lodgement, I vil give you proper drefs, den go prefent yourfelf to de fame hotels, de very fame houfe; you will find all de doors dat was fhut in your face as footman Anglois, will fly open demfelves to a French valet de chambre."

Y. Wild. Well, Papillion?

Pap. Gad, Sir, I thought it was but an honeft artifice, fo I determin'd to follow my friend's advice.

Y. Wild. Did it fucceed?

Pap. Better than expectation: My tawny face, long queu, and broken Englifh, was a pas par tout. Befides, when I am out of place, this difguife procures me many refources.

Y. Wild. As how?

P. Why, at a pinch, Sir, I am either a teacher of tongues, a frifeur, a dentift, or a dancing-mafter; thefe, Sir, are hereditary profeffions to Frenchmen. But now, Sir, to the point: As you were pleafed to be fo candid with me, I was determin'd to have no referve with you. You have ftudied books, I have ftudied men; you want advice, and I have fome at your fervice.

B 2 *Y. Wild.*

Y. Wild. Well, I'll be your cuſtomer.

Pap. But guard my ſecret : if I ſhould be ſo unfortunate to loſe your place, don't ſhut me out from every other.

Y. Wild. You may rely upon me.

Pap. In a few years I ſhall be in a condition to retire from buſineſs ; but whether I ſhall ſettle at my family-ſeat, or paſs over the continent, is as yet undetermined. Perhaps, in gratitude to the country, I may purchaſe a marquiſate near Paris, and ſpend the money I have got by their means, generouſly amongſt them.

Y. Wild. A grateful intention. But let us ſally. Where do we open ?

Pap. Let us ſee—one o'clock—it is a fine day : the Mall will be crouded.

Y. Wild. Alons.

Pap. But don't ſtare, Sir ; ſurvey every thing with an air of habit and indifference.

Y. Wild. Never fear.

Pap. But I would, Sir, crave a moment's audience, upon a ſubject that may prove very material to you.

Y. Wild. proceed.

Pap. You will pardon my preſumption ; but you have, my good maſter, one little foible that I could wiſh you to correct.

Y. Wild. What is it ?

Pap. And yet it is a pity too, you do it ſo very well.

Y. Wild. Prithee be plain.

Pap. You have, Sir, a lively imagination, with a moſt happy turn for invention.

Y. Wild. Well.

Pap. But now and then in your narratives you are hurry'd, by a flow of ſpirits, to border upon the improbable, a little given to the marvellous.

Y. Wild.

Y. Wild. I underſtand you: what, I am ſomewhat ſubject to lying.

Pap. Oh, pardon me, Sir; I don't ſay that; no, no, only a little apt to embelliſh, that's all. To be ſure it is a fine gift; that there is no diſputing: but men in general are ſo ſtupid, ſo rigorouſly attach'd to matter of fact——And yet this talent of yours is the very ſoul and ſpirit of poetry; and why it ſhould not be the ſame in proſe, I can't for my life determine.

Y. Wild. You would adviſe me, then, not to be quite ſo poetical in proſe?

Pap. Why, Sir, if you would deſcend a little to the grovelling comprehenſion of the million, I think it would be as well.

Y. Wild. I'll think of it.

Pap. Beſides, Sir, people in this town are more ſmoaky and ſuſpicious. Oxford, you know, is the ſeat of the muſes, and a man is naturally permitted more ornament and garniture to his converſation than they will allow in this latitude.

Y. Wild. I believe you are right. But we ſhall be late. D'ye hear me, Papillion: if at any time you find me growing too poetical give me a hint; your advice ſhan't be thrown away.

[*Exit.*

Pap. I wiſh it mayn't; but the diſeaſe is too rooted to be quickly removed. Lord, how I have ſweat for him! yet he is as unembarraſſed, eaſy, and fluent, all the time as if he really believed what he ſaid. Well, to be ſure he is a great maſter; it is a thouſand pities his genius could not be converted to ſome public ſervice: I think the government ſhould employ him to anſwer the Bruſſels Gazette. I'll be hanged if he is not too many for Monſieur Maubert, at his own weapons.

[*Exit.*

SCENE

THE LYAR.

SCENE the Park.

Enter Mifs GRANTAM *and* Mifs GODFREY, *and Servant.*

Mifs Grantam. John, let the chariot go round to Spring-Gardens, for your miftrefs and I fhall call at Lady Bab's, Mifs Arabella Allnight's, the Countefs of Crumple's, and the tall man's, this morning. My dear Mifs Godfrey, what trouble I have had to get you out! why, child, you are as tedious as a long morning. Do you know now, that of all places of public rendezvous I honour the Park? forty thoufand million of times preferable to the play-houfe! Don't you think fo my dear?
Mifs Godfrey. They are both well in their way.
M. Gr. Way! why the purpofe of both is the fame; to meet company, is'n't it? what, d'ye think I go there for the plays, or come here for the trees? ha! ha! well that is well enough. But, O Gemini! I beg a million of pardons: Your are a prude, and have no relifh for the little innocent liberties with which a fine woman may indulge herfelf in public.
M. God. Liberties in public!
M. Gr. Yes, child, fuch as enchoring a fong at an opera, interrupting a play in a critical fcene of diftrefs, hallooing to a pretty fellow crofs the Mall, as loud as if you were calling a coach. Why, do you know now, my dear that by a lucky ftroke in drefs, and a few high airs of my own making, I have had the good fortune to be gazed at and followed by as great a croud, on a Sunday, as if I was the Tripoly ambaffador?
M. God.

M. God. The good fortune Ma'am! Surely, the wiſh of every decent women is to be unnotic'd in public.

M. Gr. Decent! oh, my dear queer creature, what a phraſe have you found out for a woman of faſhion! Decency is, child, a mere burgeois, plebeian quality, and fit only for thoſe who pay court to the world, and not to us to whom the world pays court. Upon my word, you muſt enlarge your ideas: you are a fine girl and we muſt not have you loſt; I'll undertake you myſelf. But, as I was ſaying——Pray, my dear, what was I ſaying?

M. God. I profeſs I don't recollect.

M. Gr. Hey!—Oh, ah, the Park. One great reaſon for my loving the Park is, that one has ſo many opportunities of creating connections.

M. God. Ma'am

M. Gr. Nay, don't look grave. Why, do you know that all my male friendſhips are form'd in this place?

M. God. It is an odd ſpot: But you muſt pardon me if I doubt the poſſibility.

M. Gr. Oh, I will convince you in a moment; for here ſeems to be coming a good ſmart figure that I do'nt recollect. I will throw out a lure.

M. God. Nay, for Heaven's ſake!

M. Gr. I am detirmin'd, child: that is——

M. God. You will excuſe my withdrawing.

M. Gr. Oh, pleaſe yourſelf, my dear.

[*Exit Miſs* Godfrey.

Enter YOUNG WILDING *with* PAPILLION.

Y. Wild. Your ladyſhiy's handkerchief, Ma'am.

M. Gr. I am, Sir, concern'd at the trouble—

Y. Wild. A moſt happy incident for me, Madam; as chance has given me an honour in one

lucky

lucky minute, that the most diligent attention has not been able to procure for me in the whole tedious round of a revolving year.

M. Gr. Is this meant to me, Sir?

Y. Wild. To whom else, Madam? Surely you must have mark'd my respectful assiduity, my uninterrupted attendance; to plays, operas, balls, routs, and ridottas, I have pursued you like your shadow; I have besieged your door for a glimpse of your exit and entrance, like a distressed creditor, who has no arms against privilege but perseverance.

Pap. So, now he is in for it; stop him who can.

Y. Wild. In short, Madam, ever since I quitted America, which I take now to be about a year, I have as faithfully guarded the live-long night, your ladyship's portal, as a centinal the powder magazine in a fortified city.

Pap. Quitted America! well pull'd.

M. Gr. You have serv'd in America then?

Y. Wild Full four years Ma'am: and during that whole time, not a single action of consequence, but I had an opportunity to signalize myself; and I think I may, without vanity, affirm, I did not miss the occasion. You have heard of Quebec, I presume?

Pap. What the deuce is he driving at now?

Y. Wild. The project to surprize that place was thought a happy expedient, and the first mounting the breach a gallant exploit. There, indeed, the whole army did me justice.

M. Gr. I have heard the honour of that conquest attributed to another name.

Y. Wild. The mere taking the town, Ma'am. But that's a trifle: sieges now a-days are reduc'd to certainties; it is amazing how mi-
nutely

nutely exact we, who knew the bufinefs are at calculation: for inftance now, we will fuppofe the commander in chief, addreffing himfelf to me, was to fay, " Colonel, I want to reduce that fortrefs ; what will be the expence?" " Why, pleafe your highnefs, the reduction of that fortrefs will coft you one thoufand and two lives, fixty-nine legs, ditto arms, fourfcore fractures, with about twenty dozen of flefh wounds."

M. Gr. And you fhall be near the mark?

Y. Wild. To an odd joint, Ma'am. But, Madam, it is not to the French alone that my feats are confin'd: Cherokees, Catabaws, with all the Aws and Ees of the continent, have felt the force of my arms.

Pap. This is too much, Sir.

Y. Wild. Hands off! Nor am I lefs adroit at a treaty, Madam, than terrible in battle. To me we owe the friendfhip of the Five Nations, and I had the firft honour of fmoaking the pipe of peace with the little Carpenter.

M. Gr. And fo young!

Y. Wild. This gentleman, though a Frenchman and an enemy, I had the fortune to deliver from the Mohawks, whofe prifoner he had been for nine years. He gives a moft entertaining account of their laws and cuftoms : he fhall prefent you with the wampum belt, and a fcalping-knife. Will you permit him, Madam, juft to give you a tafte of the military dance, with a fhort fpecimen of their warhoop.

Pap. For Heaven's fake!

M. Gr. The place is too public.

Y. Wild. In fhort, Madam, after having gathered as many laurels abroad as would garnifh a Gothic cathedral at Chriftmas, I returned to reap the harveft of the well-fought field. Here it was my my good fortune to encounter you: then was the victor vanquished; what the enemy could never accomplish, your eyes in an inftant atchiev'd; prouder to ferve here than command in chief elfewhere; and more glorious in wearing your chains, than in triumphing over the vanquifh'd world.

M. Gr. I have got here a moft heroical lover: But I fee Sir James Elliot coming, and muft difmifs him [*Afide*] Well, Sir, I accept the tender of your paffion, and may find a time to renew our acquaintance; at prefent it is neceffary we fhould feparate.

Y. Wild. " Slave to your will, I live but to obey you." But may I be indulged with the knowledge of your refidence.

M. Gr. Sir?

Y. Wild. Your place of above.

M. Gr. Oh, Sir, you can't want to be acquainted with that; you have a whole year ftood centinel at my ladyfhip's portal.

Y. Wild. Madam, I—I—I—

M. Gr. Oh, Sir, your fervant. Ha, ha, ha! What, you are caught! Ha, ha, ha! Well, he has a more intrepid affurance. Adieu, my Mars. Ha, ha, ha! [*Exit.*

Pap. That laft was an unlucky queftion, Sir.

Y. Wild. A little mal-a-propos I muft confefs.

Pap. A man fhould have a good memory who deals much in this poetical profe.

Y. Wild. Poh! I'll foon re-eftablifh my credit. But I muft know who this girl is: Hark ye, Papillion, could not you contrive to pump out of her footman—I fee there he ftands—the name of his miftrefs?

Pap. I will try. [*Exit.*

[Wilding *retires to the back of the ftage.*

Enter

Enter Sir JAMES ELLIOT, *and Servant.*
Sir James. Mufic and an entertainment?
Servant. Yes, Sir.
Sir Ja. Laſt night, upon the water?
Serv. Upon the water, laſt night.
Sir Ja. Who gave it?
Serv. That, Sir, I can't ſay.

To them WILDING.

Y. Wild. Sir James Elliot your moſt devoted.
Sir Ja. Ah, my dear Wilding! you are welcome to town.
Y. Wilding. You will pardon my impatience; I interrupted you; you ſeem'd upon an intereſting ſubject.
Sir Ja. Oh, an affair of gallantry.
Y. Wild. Of what kind?
Sir. Ja. A young lady regal'd laſt night by her lover, on the Thames.
Y. Wild. As how?
Sir Ja. A band of mufic in boats.
Y. Wild. Were they good performers?
Sir Ja. The beſt. Then conducted to Marble-hall, where ſhe found a magnificent collation.
Y. Wild. Well order'd?
Sir Ja. With elegance. After ſupper a ball; and to conclude the night, a firework.
Y. Wild. Was the laſt well deſign'd?
Sir Ja. Superb.
Y. Wild. And happily executed?
Sir Ja. Not a ſingle faux pas.
Y. Wild. And you don't know who gave it?
Sir Ja. I can't even gueſs.
Y. Wild. Ha, ha, ha!
Sir. Ja. Why do you laugh?
Y. Wild. Ha, ha, ha! It was me.

Sir Ja. You!
Pap. You, Sir!
Y. Wild. Moi—me.
Pap. So, fo, fo; he is enter'd again.
Sir Ja. Why, you are fortunate, to find a miftrefs in fo fhort a fpace of time.
Y. Wild. Short! why, man, I have been in London thefe fix weeks.
Pap. O Lord, O Lord!
Y. Wild. It is true, not caring to encounter my father, I have rarely ventur'd out but at nights.
Pap. I can hold no longer. Dear Sir.
Y. Wild. Peace, puppy!
Pap. A curb to your poetical vein.
Y. Wild. I fhall curb your impertinence.— But fince the ftory is got abroad I will, my dear friend, treat you with all the particulars.
Sir Ja. I fhall hear it with pleafure.—This is a lucky adventure: But he muft not know he is my rival. [*Afide*]
Y. Wild. Why, Sir, between fix and feven my goddefs embark'd at Somerfet-ftairs, in one of the companies barges, gilt and hung with damafk, exprefly for the occafion.
Pap. Mercy on us!
Y. Wild. At the cabin-door fhe was accofted by a beautiful boy, who, in the garb of a Cupid, paid her fome compliments in verfe of my own compofing: the conceits were pretty; allufions to Venus and the fea—the lady and the Thames —no great matter; but, however, well-tim'd, and what was better, well taken.
Sir. Ja. Doubtlefs.
Pap. At what a rate he runs!
Y. Wild. As foon as we had gained the center of the river, two boats full of trumpets, French
horns,

horns, and other martial mufic, ftruck up their
fprightly ftrains from the Surry-fide, which were
echo'd by a fuitable number of lutes, flutes,
and hautboys from the oppofite fhore. In this
ftate, the oars keeping time, we majeftically
fail'd along, till the arches of the New Bridge
gave a paufe, and an opportunity for an elegant
defart in Drefden china, by Robinfon. Here the
repaft clos'd, with a few favourite airs from Eliza,
Tenducci, and the Mattei.

Pap. Mercy on us!

Y. Wild. Oppofite Lambeth I had prepared a
naval engagement, in which Bofcawen's victory
over the French was repeated: the action was
conducted by one of the commanders on that expedition, and not a fingle incident omitted.

Sir Ja. Surely you exaggerate a little.

Pap. Yes, yes, this battle will fink him.

Y. Wild. True to the letter, upon my honour,
I fha'n't trouble you with a repetition of our
collation, ball, feu d'artifice, with the thoufand
little incidental amufements that chance or defign
produc'd; it is a enough to know, that all that
could flatter the fenfes, fire the imagination, or
gratify the expectation, was there produc'd in a
lavifh abundance.

Sir Ja. The facrifice was, I prefume, grateful
to your deity.

Y. Wild. Upon that fubject you muft pardon
my filence.

Pap. Modeft creature!

Sir Ja. I wifh you joy of your fuccefs.---For
the prefent you will excufe me.

Y. Wild. Nay, but ftay and hear the conclufion.

Sir Ja. For that I fhall feize another occafion.   [*Exit.*

Pap. Nobly perform'd, Sir.

Y. Wild.

Y. Wild. Yes, I think happily hit off.

Pap. May I take the liberty to offer one queftion?

Y. Wild. Freely.

Pap. Pray, Sir, are you often vifited with thefe waking dreams?

Y. Wild. Dreams! what doft mean by dreams?

Pap. Thefe ornamental reveries, thefe frolics of fancy, which, in the judgment of the vulgar, would be deem'd abfolute flames.

Y. Wild. Why, Papillion, you have but a poor, narrow, circumfcribed genius.

Pap. I muft own, Sir, I have no fublimity fufficient to relifh the full fire of your Pindaric mufe.

Y. Wild. No; a plebeian foul! But I will animate thy clay: mark my example, follow my fteps, and in time thou may'ft rival thy mafter.

Pap. Never, never, Sir, I have no talents to fight battles without blows, and give feafts that don't coft me a farthing. Befides, Sir, to what purpofe are all thefe embellifhments? Why tell the lady you have been in London a year?

Y. Wild. The better to plead the length, and confequently the ftrength of my paffion.

Pap. But why, Sir, a foldier.

Y. Wild. How little thou know'ft of the fex! What, I fuppofe thou would'ft have me attack them in mood and figure, by a pedantic, claffical quotation, or a pompous parade of jargon from the fchools. What, doft think that women are to be got like degrees?

Pap. Nay, Sir———

Y. Wild. No, no; the fcavoir vivre is the fcience for them; the man of war is their man: they muft be taken like towns, by lines of approach, counterfcarps, angles, trenches, cohorns,

and

and covert-ways; then enter sword in hand, pell-mell! oh, how they melt at the Gothic names of General Swappinback, Count Roufoumoufky, Prince Montecuculi, and Marfhal Fuftinburgh! Men may fay what they will of their Ovid, their Petrarch, and their Waller, but I'll undertake to do more bufinefs by the fingle aid of the London Gazette, than by all the fighing, dying, crying crochets, that the whole race of rhymers have ever produced.

Pap. Very well, Sir; this is all very lively; but remember the travelling pitcher: if you don't one time or other, under favour, lye yourfelf into fome confounded fcrape, I will content to be hanged.

Y. Wild. Do you think fo, Papillion?—And whenever that happens, if I don't lye myfelf out of it again, why then I will be content to be cruci-fy'd. And fo, along after the lady. [*Stops fhort, going out.*] Zounds, here comes my father! I muft fly. Watch him, Papillion, and bring me word to the Cardigan.

[*Exeunt feparately.*

END of the FIRST ACT.

ACT II.

SCENE. A TAVERN.

YOUNG WILDING *and* PAPILLION *rising from Table.*

Young Wilding.

GAD, I had like to have run into the old gentleman's mouth.

Pap. It is pretty near the same thing; for I saw him join Sir James Elliot: so your arrival is no longer a secret.

Y. Wild. Why then I must lose my pleasure, and you your preferment: I must submit to the dull decency of a sober family, and you to the customary duties of brushing and powdering. But I was so flutter'd at meeting my father, that I forgot the fair; pr'ythee who is she?

Pap. There were two.

Y. Wild. That I saw?

Pap. From her footman I learnt her name was Godfrey.

Y. Wild. And her fortune!

Pap. Immense.

Y. Wild. Single, I hope?

Pap. Certainly

Pap. Then will I have her.

Pap. What, whether she will or no?

Y. Wild. Yes.

Pap. How will you manage that?

Y. Wild.

Y. Wild. By making it impoſſible for her to marry any one elſe.

Pap. I don't underſtand you, Sir.

Y. Wild. Oh, I ſhall only have recourſe to that talent you ſo mightily admire. You will ſee, by the circulation of a few anecdotes, how ſoon I will get rid of my rivals.

Pap. At the expence of the lady's reputation, perhaps.

Y. Wild. That will be as it happens.

Pap. And have you no qualms, Sir?

Y. Wild. Why, where's the injury?

Pap. No injury to ruin her fame!

Y. Wild. I will reſtore it to her again.

Pap. How?

Y. Wild. Turn tinker and mend it myſelf.

Pap. Which way?

Y. Wild. The old way; ſolder it by marriage: that, you know, is the modern ſalve for every ſore.

Enter WAITER.

Wait. An elderly gentleman to enquire for Mr Wilding.

Y. Wild. For me! what ſort of a being is it?

Wait. Being, Sir!

Y. Wild. Ay; how is he dreſt?

Wait. In a tye-wig and ſnuff-colour'd coat.

Pap. Zooks, Sir, it is your father.

Y. Wild. Shew him up. [*Exit* Waiter.

Pap. And what muſt I do?

Y. Wild. Recover your broken Engliſh, but preſerve your rank: I have a reaſon for it.

Enter OLD WILDING.

O. Wild. Your ſervant, Sir: your are welcome to town.

D *Y. Wild.*

Y. Wild. You have juſt prevented me, Sir: I was preparing to pay my duty to you.

O. Wild. If you thought it a duty, you ſhould, I think, have ſooner diſcharg'd it.

Y. Wild. Sir!

O. Wild. Was it quite ſo decent, Jack, to be ſix weeks in town, and conceal yourſelf only from me?

Y. Wild. Six weeks! I have ſcarce been ſix hours.

O. Wild. Come, come, I am better inform'd.

Y. Wild. Indeed, Sir, you are impos'd upon. This gentleman (who firſt give me leave to have the honour of introducing to you), this, Sir, is the marquis de Chatteau Briant, of an ancient houſe in Brittany; who, travelling through England, choſe to make Oxford for ſome time the place of his reſidence, where I had the happineſs of his acquaintance.

O. Wild. Does he ſpeak Engliſh.

Y. Wild. Not fluently, but underſtands it perfectly.

Pap. Pray, Sir,——

O. Wild. Any ſervices, Sir, that I can render you here you may readily command.

Pap. Beacoup d'honeur.

Y. Wild. This gentleman, I ſay, Sir, whoſe quality and country are ſufficient ſecurities for his veracity, will aſſure you that yeſterday we left Oxford together.

O. Wild. Indeed!

Pap. C'eſt vrai.

O. Wild. This is amazing, I was, at the ſame time, inform'd of another circumſtance too, that, I confeſs, made me a little uneaſy, as it interfer'd with a favourite ſcheme of my own.

Y. Wild.

Y. Wild. What could that be, pray, Sir?

O. Wild. That you had conceiv'd a violent affection for a fair lady.

Y. Wild. Sir!

O. Wild. And had given her very gallant and very expenfive proofs of your paffion.

Y. Wild. Me, Sir!

O. Wild. Particularly laft night; mufic, colla-tions, balls, and fireworks.

Y. Wild. Monfieur le marquis!—And pray, Sir, who could tell you all this?

O. Wild. An old friend of yours.

Y. Wild. His name, if you pleafe.

O. Wild. Sir James Elliot.

Y. Wild. Yes: I thought he was the man.

O. Wild. Your reafon.

Y. Wild. Why, Sir, though Sir James Elliot, has a great many good qualities, and is, upon the whole, a valuable man, yet he has one fault which has long determined me to drop his acquaintance.

O. Wild. What may that be?

Y. Wild. Why you can't, Sir, be a ftranger to his prodigious fkill in the traveller's talent.

O. Wild. How!

Y. Wild. Oh, notorious to a proverb.——His friends, who are tender of his fame, glofs over his foible, by calling him an agreeable novelift: and fo he is, with a vengeance: Why, he will tell you more lyes in an hour, than all the circulating libraries, put together, will publifh in a year.

O. Wild. Indeed!

Y. Wild. Oh, he is the modern Mandeville at Oxford; he was always diftinguifh'd by the facetious appellation of the Bouncer.

O. Wild. Amazing!

D 2 *Y. Wild.*

Y. Wild. Lord, Sir, he is so well understood in his own country, that at the last Hereford assize a cause, as clear as the sun, was absolutely thrown away by his being merely mentioned as a witness.

O. Wild. A strange turn.

Y. Wild Unaccountable. But there I think they went a little too far; for if it had come to an oath, I don't think he would have bounc'd neither; but in common occurrences there is no repeating after him. Indeed, my great reason for dropping him was, that my credit began to be a little suspected too.

Pap. Poor gentleman!

O. Wild. Why, I never heard this of him.

Y. Wild. That may be: but can there be a stronger proof of his practice than the flam he has been telling you, of fireworks, and the Lord knows what. And I dare swear, Sir, he was very fluent and florid in his description.

O. Wild. Extremely.

Y. Wild. Yes, that is just his way; and not a syllable of truth from the beginning to the ending, marquis?

Pap. Oh, dat is all a fiction upon mine honour.

Y. Wild. You see, Sir.

O. Wild. Clearly. I really can't help pitying the poor man. I have heard of people, who, by long habit, become a kind of constitutional lyars.

Y. Wild. Your observation is just; that is exactly his case.

Pap. I'm sure it is your's.

O. Wild. Well; Sir, I suppose we shall see you this evening.

Y. Wild.

Y. Wild. The marquis has an appointment with some of his countrymen, which I have promis'd to attend; besides, Sir, as he is an entire stranger in town, he may want my little services.

O. Wild. Where can I see you in about an hour? I have a short visit to make, in which you are deeply concern'd.

Y. Wild. I shall attend your commands; but where?

O. Wild. Why here. Marquis, I am your obedient servant.

Pap. Votre serviteur tres humble.

[*Exit* Old Wilding.

Y. Wild. So, Papillion; that difficulty is dispatch'd. I think I am even with Sir James for his tattling.

Pap. Most ingeniously manag'd: But are not you afraid of the consequence?

Y. Wild. I do not comprehend you.

Pap. A future explanation between the parties.

Y. Wild. That may embarrass: but the day is distant. I warrant I will bring myself off.

Pap. It is in vain for me to advise.

Y. Wild. Why, to say truth, I do begin to find my system attended with danger: Give me your hand, Papillion—I will reform.

Pap. Ah, Sir!

Y. Wild. I positively will: Why this practice may in time destroy my credit.

Pap. That is pretty well done already. [*Aside.*] Ay, think of that, Sir.

Y. Wild. Well, if I don't turn out the meerest dull matter of fact fellow——But, Papillion, I must scribble a billet to my new flame. I think her name is——

Pap.

Pap. Godfrey; her father, an Indian governor, shut up in the strong room at Calcutta, left her all his wealth: she lives near miss Grantam, by Grosvenor-square.

Y. Wild. A governor!—oh ho!—Bushels of rupees, and pecks of pagodas, I reckon.—— Well, I long to be rumaging.—But the old gentleman will soon return: I will hasten to finish my letter.—But, Papillion, what could my father mean by a visit in which I am deeply concern'd?

Pap. I can't guess.

Y. Wild. I shall know presently.——To Miss Godfrey, formerly of Calcutta, now residing in Grosvenor-square.—Papillion, I won't tell her a word of a lye.

Pap. You won't, Sir?

Y. Wild. No; it would be ungenerous to deceive a lady. No; I will be open, candid and sincere.

Pap. And if you are, it will be the first time.

[*Exeunt.*

Enter Miss GRANTAM *and Miss* GODFREY.

M. God. And you really like this gallant spark?

M. Gr. Prodigiously. Oh, I'm quite in love with his assurance! I wonder who he is: he can't have been long in town: a young fellow of his easy impudence must have soon made his way to the best of company.

M. God. By way of amusement he may prove no disagreeable acquaintance; but you can't, surely, have any serious designs upon him.

M. Gr. Indeed but I have.

M. God.

M. God. And poor Sir James Elliot is to be discarded at once?

M. Gr. Oh, no.

M. God. What is your intention in regard to him?

M. Gr. Hey?—I can't tell you. Perhaps, if I don't like this new man better, I may marry him.

M. God. Thou art a strange giddy girl.

M. Gr. Quite the reverse; a perfect pattern of prudence: why, would you have me less careful of my person than my purse?

M. God. My dear!

M. Gr. Why I say, child, my fortune being in money, I have some in India-bonds, some in the Bank, some on this loan, some on the other; so that if one fun fails, I have a sure resource in the rest.

M. God. Very true.

M. Gr. Well, my dear, just so I manage my love-affairs: if I should not like this man—if he should not like me—if we should quarrel—if, if —or in short, if any of the ifs should happen; which you know break engagements every day, why by this means I shall never be at a loss.

M. God. Quite provident. Well, and pray on how many different securities have you at present plac'd out your love?

M. Gr. Three: the sober Sir James Elliot, the new America-man, and this morning I expected a formal proposal from an old friend of my father.

M. God. Mr. Wilding.

M. Gr. Yes; but I don't reckon much upon him: for you know, my dear, what can I do with an aukward, raw, college cub? Though,

upon

upon second thoughts, that may'nt be too bad neither; for as I muſt have the faſhioning of him, he may be eaſily moulded to one's mind.'

Enter a SERVANT.

Serv. Mr. Wilding, Madam.

M. Gr. Shew him in. [*Exit* Servant.] You need not go, my dear; we have no particular buſineſs.

M. God. I wonder now what ſhe calls particular buſineſs.

Enter OLD WILDING.

O. Wild. Ladies your ſervant. I wait upon you, Madam, with a requeſt from my ſon, that he may be permitted the honour of kiſſing your had.

M. Gr. Your ſon is in town then?

O. Wild. He came laſt night, Ma'am; and though but juſt from the univerſity I think I may venture to affirm, with as little the air of a pedant as——

M. Gr. I don't, Mr. Wilding, queſtion the accompliſhments of your ſon; and ſhall own too, that his being deſcended from the old friend of my father, is to me the ſtrongeſt recommendation.

O. Wild. You honour me, Madam.

M. Gr. But, Sir, I have ſomething to ſay——

O. Wild. Pray, Madam, ſpeak out; it is impoſſible to be too explicit on theſe important occaſions.

M. Gr. Why then, Sir, to a man of your wiſdom and experience I need not obſerve, that the loſs of a parent to counſel and direct at this ſolemn

lemn crisis, has made a greater degree of personal prudence necessary in me.

O. Wild. Perfectly right, Ma'am.

M. Gr. We live, Sir, in a very censorious world; a young woman can't be too much upon her guard; nor should I chuse to admit any man in the quality of a lover, if there was not at least a strong probability——

O. Wild. Of a more intimate connection. I hope, Madam, you have heard nothing to the disadvantage of my son.

M. Gr. Not a syllable: but you know, Sir, there are such things in nature as unaccountable antipathies, aversions, that we take at first sight: I should be glad there could be no danger of that.

O. Wild. I understand you, Madam; you shall have all the satisfaction imaginable: Jack is to meet me immediately: I will conduct him under your window; and if his figure has the misfortune to displease, I will take care his addresses shall never offend you. Your most obedient servant. *Exit.*]

M. Gr. Now there is a polite, sensible, old father for you.

M. God. Yes; and a very discreet, prudent daughter he is likely to have. Oh, you are a great hypocrite, Kitty.

Enter a SERVANT.

Serv. A letter to you, Madam. [*To Miss* Godfrey.] Sir James Elliot to wait on your ladyship. [*To Miss* Grantam.] *Exit.*

M. Gr. Lord, I hope he won't stay long here. He comes and seems intirely wrapt up in the dismals: what can be the matter now?

E *Enter*

Enter Sir JAMES ELLIOT.

Sir Ja. In paſſing by your door, I took the liberty, Ma'am, of enquiring after your health.

M. Gr. Very obliging. I hope, Sir, you receiv'd a favourable account.

Sir Ja. I did not know but you might have caught cold laſt night.

M. Gr. Cold! why Sir, I hope I did not ſleep with my bed-chamber window open.

Sir Ja. Ma'am!

M. Gr. Sir!

Sir Ja. No, Ma'am; but it was rather hazardous to ſtay ſo late upon the water.

M. Gr. Upon the water!

Sir Ja. Not but the variety of amuſements, it muſt be own'd, were a ſufficient temptation.

M. Gr. What can he be driving at now!

Sir Ja. And pray, Madam, what think you of Young Wilding? is not he a gay, agreeable, ſprightly——

M. Gr. I never give my opinion of people I don't know.

Sir Ja. You don't know him!

M. Gr. No.

Sir Ja. And his father I did not meet at your door!

M. Gr. Moſt likely you did.

Sir Ja. I am glad you own that, however: But, for the ſon, you never——

M. Gr. Sat eyes upon him.

Sir Ja. Really?

M. Gr. Really.

Sir Ja. Finely ſupported. Now, Madam, do you know that one of us is juſt going to make a very ridiculous figure?

M. Gr.

M. Ge. Sir, I never had the leaſt doubt of your talents for excelling in that way.

Sir Ja. Ma'am, you do me honour: but it does not happen to fall to my lot upon this occaſion, however.

M. Gr. And that is a wonder!—What, then I am to be the fool of the comedy, I ſuppoſe.

Sir Ja. Admirably rally'd! But I ſhall daſh the ſpirit of that triumphant laugh.

M. Gr. I dare the attack. Come on, Sir.

Sir Ja. Known then, and bluſh, if you are not as loſt to ſhame as dead to decency, that I am no ſtranger to all laſt night's tranſactions.

M. Gr. Indeed!

Sir Ja. From your firſt entering the barge at Somerſet-houſe, to your laſt landing at Whitehall.

M. Gr. Surprizing!

Sir Ja. Cupids, collations, feaſts, fireworks, all have reach'd me.

M. Gr. Why you deal in magic.

Sir Ja. My intelligence is as natural as it is infallible.

M. Gr. May I be indulg'd with the name of your informer.

Sir Ja. Freely, Madam. Only the very individual ſpark to whoſe folly you were indebted for this gallant profuſion.

M. Gr. But his name?

Sir Ja. Young Wilding.

M. Gr. You had this ſtory from him?

Sir Ja. I had.

M. Gr. From Wilding!—That is amazing.

Sir Ja. Oh ho! what you are confounded at laſt; and no evaſion to ſubterfuge, no——

M. Gr. Lookye, Sir James; what you can mean by this ſtrange ſtory, and very extraordinary

nary behaviour, it is impoſſible for me to conceive; but if it is meant as an artifice to palliate your infidelity to me, leſs pains would have anſwer'd your purpoſe.

Sir Ja. Oh, Madam, I know you are provided.

M. Gr. Matchleſs inſolence! as you can't expect that I ſhould be prodigiouſly pleas'd with the ſubject of this viſit, you won't be ſurprized at my wiſhing it as ſhort as poſſible.

Sir Ja. I don't wonder you feel pain at my preſence: but you may reſt ſecure you will have no interruption for me; and I really think it would be pity to part two people ſo exactly formed for each other. Your ladyſhip's ſervant. [*Going.*] But, Madam, though your ſex ſecures you from any farther reſentment, yet the preſent object of your favour may have ſomething to fear.
[*Exit.*

M. Gr. Very well. Now my dear I hope you will acknowledge the prudence of my plan. To what a pretty condition I muſt have been reduc'd if my hopes had reſted upon one lover alone.

M. God. But are you ſure that your method to multiply, may not be the means to reduce the number of your ſlaves?

M. Gr. Impoſſible!—Why can't you diſcern that this flam of Sir James Elliot's is a mere fetch to favour his retreat.

M. God. And you never ſaw Wilding?

M. Gr. Never.

M. God. There is ſome myſtery in this. I have too here in my hand another mortification that you muſt endure.

M. Gr. Of what kind?

M. God.

M. God. A little ally'd to the laſt: it is from the military ſpark you met this morning.

M. Gr. What are the contents?

M. God. Only a formal declaration of love.

M. Gr. Why, you did not ſee him.

M. God. But it ſeems he did me.

M. Gr. Might I peruſe it?—" Battles—no wounds ſo fatal—cannon-balls—Cupid—ſpring a mine—cruelty—die on a counterſcrap—eyes—artillery—death the ſtranger." It is addreſs'd to you.

M. God. I told you ſo.

M. Gr. You will pardon me, my dear; but I really can't compliment you upon the ſuppoſition of a conqueſt at my expence.

M. God. That would be enough to make me vain: But why do you think it was ſo impoſſible?

M. Gr. And do you poſitively want a reaſon?

M. God. Poſitively.

M. Gr. Why, then I ſhall refer you for an anſwer to a faithful counſellor and moſt accompliſh'd critic.

M. God. Who may that be?

M. Gr. The mirror upon your toilette.

M. God. Perhaps you may differ in judgment.

M. Gr. Why, can glaſſes flatter?

M. God. I can't ſay I think that neceſſary.

M. Gr. Saucy enough!—But come, child, don't let us quarrel upon ſo whimſical an occaſion; time will explain the whole. You will favour me with your opinion of Young Wilding, at my window.

M. God. I attend you.

M. Gr. You will forgive me, my dear, the little hint I dropt; it was meant merely to ſerve you: for indeed, child, there is no quality ſo inſufferable fufferable in a young woman as felf-conceit and vanity.

M. God. You are moft prodigioufly obliging.

M. Gr. I'll follow you, Mifs. [*Exit Mifs* Godfrey.] Pert thing!—She grows immoderately ugly. I always thought her aukward, but fhe is now an abfolute fright.

M. God. [*within.*] Mifs, Mifs Grantam, your hero's at hand.

M. Gr. I come.

M. God. As I live, the very individual ftranger.

M. Gr. No, fure!—Oh Lord, let me have a peep.

M. God. It is he, it is he, it is he.

Enter OLD WILDING, YOUNG WILDING, *and* PAPILLION.

O. Wild. There, Marquis, you muft pardon me; for though Paris be more compact, yet furely London covers a much greater quantity,— Oh, Jack, look at that corner houfe: how d'ye like it?

Y. Wild. Very well: but I don't fee any thing extraordinary.

O. Wild. I wifh though you were the mafter of what it contains.

Y. Wild. What may that be, Sir?

O. Wild. The miftrefs, you rogue, you: a fine girl, and an immenfe fortune; aye, and a prudent fenfible wench into the bargain.

Y. Wild. Time enough yet, Sir.

O. Wild. I don't fee that: You are, lad, the laft of our race, and I fhould be glad to fee fome probability of its continuance.

Y. Wild.

Y. Wild. Suppose, Sir, you were to repeat your endeavours, you have cordially my consent.

O. Wild. No; rather too late in life for that experiment.

Y. Wild. Why, Sir, would you recommend a condition to me, that you disapprove of yourself.

O. Wild. Why, Sirrah, I have done my duty to the public and my family, by producing you: now, Sir, it is incumbent on you to discharge your debt.

Y. Wild. In the college cant, I shall beg leave to tick a little longer.

O. Wild. Why then, to be serious son, this is the very business I wanted to talk with you about. In a word, I wish you married; and by providing the lady of that mansion for the purpose, I have proved myself both a father and a friend.

Y. Wild. Far be it from me to question your care; yet some preparation for so important a change——

O. Wild. Oh, I will allow you a week.

Y. Wild. A little more knowledge of the world.

O. Wild. That you may study at leisure.

Y. Wild. Now all Europe is in arms, my design was to serve my country abroad.

O. Wild. You will be full as useful to it by recruiting her subjects at home.

Y Wild. You are then resolv'd.

O. Wild. Fix'd.

Y. Wild. Positively?

O. Wild. Peremptorily.

Y. Wild. No prayers——

O. Wild. Can move me.

Y. Wild. How the deuce shall I get out of this toil. [*Aside*] But suppose, Sir, there should be an unsurmountable objection?

O. Wild.

O. Wild. Oh, leave the reconciling that to me; I am an excellent cafuift.

Y. Wild. But, I fay, Sir, if it fhould be impoffible to obey your commands?

O. Wild. Impoffible!—I don't underftand you.

Y. Wild. Oh, Sir!—But, on my knees, firft let me crave your pardon.

O. Wild. Pardon! for what?

Y. Wild. I fear I have loft all title to your future favour.

O. Wild. Which way?

Y. Wild. I have done a deed——

O. Wild. Let us hear it.

Y. Wild. At Abington, in the county of Berks:

O. Wild. Well?

Y. Wild. I am——

O. Wild. What?

Y. Wild. Already married.

O. Wild. Married!

Pap. Married!

Y. Wild. Married.

O. Wild. And without my confent?

Y. Wild. Compell'd; fatally forc'd. Oh, Sir, did you but know all the circumftances of my fad, fad ftory, your rage would foon convert itfelf to pity.

O. Wild. What an unluckly event!—But rife, and let me hear it all.

Y. Wild. The fhame and confufion I now feel renders that tafk at prefent impoffible: I therefore rely for the relation on the good offices of this faithful friend.

Pap. Me, Sir, I never heard one word of the matter.

O. Wild. Come, Marquis, favour me with the particulars.

Pap.

Pap. Upon my vard, Sire, dis affair has fo fhock me, that I am almoft as incapable to tell de tale as your fon.—[*To* Young Wilding.] Dry a your tears. What can I fay, Sir?

Y. Wild. Any thing.—Oh! (*Seems to weep.*)

Pap. You fee, Sire.

O. Wild. Your kind concern at the misfortunes of my family calls for the moft grateful acknowledgement.

Pap. Dis is great misfortunes, fans doute.

Y. Wild. But if you, a ftranger, are thus affected, what muft a father feel?

Pap. Oh, beaucoup great deal more.

O. Wild. But fince the evil is without a remedy, let us know the worft at once. Well, Sir, at Abington.

Pap. Yes, at Abington.

O. Wild. In the county of Berks.

Pap. Dat is right, in de county of Berks.

Y. Wild. Oh, ho!

O. Wild. Ah, Jack, Jack, are all my hopes then———Though I dread to afk, yet it muft be known; who is the girl, pray Sir?

Pap. De girl, Sir—[*Afide to* Young Wilding.] Who fhall I fay?

Y. Wild. Any body.

Pap. For de girl, I can't fay upon my vard.

O. Wild. Her condition?

Pap. Pas grande condition; dat is to be fure. But dere is no help.—[*Afide to* Young Wilding.] Sir, I am quite aground.

O. Wild. Yes; I read my fhame in his referve: fome artful huffy?

Pap. Dat may be. Vat you call huffy?

O. Wild. Or perhaps fome common creature! But I'am prepar'd to hear the worft.

Pap.

Pap. Have you no mercy?

Y. Wild. I'll step to your relief, Sir.

Pap. O Lord! a happy deliverance.

Y. Wild. Though it is almost death for me to speak, yet it would be infamous to let the reputation of that lady suffer by my silence: She is, Sir, of an ancient house and unblemish'd character.

O. Wild. That is something.

Y. Wild. And though her fortune may not be equal to the warm wishes of a fond father, yet——

O. Wild. Her name?

Y. Wild. Miss Lydia Sybthorp.

O. Wild. Sybthorp.——I never heard of that name. But proceed.

Y. Wild. The latter end of last long vacation, I went with Sir James Elliot to pass a few days at a new perchase of his near Abington. There at an assembly it was my chance to meet and dance with this lady.

O. Wild. Is she handsome?

Y. Wild. Oh, Sir, more heautiful——

O. Wild. Nay, no raptures; but go on.

Y. Wild. But to her beauty she adds politeness, affability, and discretion; unless she forfeited that character by fixing her affection on me.

O. Wilding. Modestly observed.

Y. Wild. I was deterr'd from a public declaration of my passion, dreading the scantiness of her fortune would prove an objection to you. Some private interviews she permitted.

O. Wild. Was that so decent?—But love and prudence, madness and reason.

Y. Wild.

Y. Wild. One fatal evening, the twentieth of September, if I miſtake not, we were in a retir'd room, innocently exchanging mutual vows, when her father, whom we expected to ſup abroad, came ſuddenly upon us. I had juſt time to conceal myſelf in a cloſet.

O. Wild. What, unobſerved by him?

Y. Wild. Entirely. But, as my ill ſtars would have it, a cat of whom my wife is vaſtly fond, had a few days before lodged a litter of kittens in the ſame place: I unhappily trod upon one of the brood, which ſo provok'd the implacable mother, that ſhe flew at me with the fury of a tyger.

O. Wild. I have obſerved thoſe creatures very fierce in defence of their young.

Pap. I ſhall hate a cat as long as I live.

Y. Wild. The noiſe rous'd the old gentleman's attention; he opened the door, and there diſcover'd your ſon.

Pap. Unlucky.

Y. Wild. I ruſh'd to the door; but fatally my foot ſlipt at the top of the ſtairs, and down I came tumbling to the bottom; the piſtol in my had went off by accident: this alarm'd her three brothers in the parlour, who, with all their ſervants, ruſh'd with united force upon me.

O. Wild. And ſo ſurpriz'd you?

Y. Wild. No, Sir; with my ſword I for ſome time made a gallant defence, and ſhould have inevitably eſcap'd, but a raw-bon'd, over-grown, clumſy cook-wench, ſtruck at my ſword with a kitchen poker, broke it in two, and compell'd me to ſurrender at diſcretion; the conſequence of which is obvious enough.

O. Wild.

O. Wild. Natural. The lady's reputation, your condition, her beauty, your love, all combin'd to make marriage an unavoidable meafure.

Y. Wild. May I hope then you rather think me unfortunate than culpable?

O. Wild. Why your fituation is a fufficient excufe: all I blame you for is your keeping it a fecret from me. With Mifs Grantam I fhall make an aukward figure: but the beft apology is the truth: I'll haften and explain it to her all——— Oh, Jack, Jack, this is a mortifying bufinefs.

Y. Wild. Moft melancholy.

[*Exit* Old Wilding.

Pap. I am amaz'd Sir, that you have fo carefully conceal'd this tranfaction from me.

Y. Wild. Heyday! what do you believe it too?

Pap. Believe it! Why is not the ftory of the marriage true?

Y Wild. Not a fyllable.

Pap. And the cat, and the piftol, and the poker.

Y. Wild. All invention. And were you really taken in?

Pap. Lord, Sir, how was it poffible to avoid it? Mercy on us! what a collection of circumftances have you crowded together!

Y. Wild. Genius; the mere effects of genius, Papillion. But to deceive you, who fo thoroughly know me!

Pap. But to prevent that for the future, could you not juft give your humble fervant a hint, when you are bent upon bouncing. Befides, Sir, if you recollect your fix'd refolution to reform—

Y. Wild.

Y. Wild. Ay, as to matter of fancy, the mere fport and frolic of invention; but in cafe of neceffity—why, Mifs Godfrey was at ftake, and I was forc'd to ufe all my fineffe.

Enter a SERVANT.

Serv. Two letters, Sir. [*Exit.*
Pap. There are two things in my confcience my mafter will never want: a prompt lie and a ready excufe for telling of it.
Y. Wild. Hum! bufinefs begins to thicken upon us: a challenge from Sir James Elliot, and a rendezvous from the pretty Mifs Godfrey. They fhall both be obferv'd, but in their order: therefore the lady firft. Let me fee—I have not been twenty hours in town, and I have already got a challenge, a miftrefs, and a wife; now if I can but get engaged in a chancery fuit, I fhall have my hands pretty full of employment. Come, Papillion, we have no time to be idle.

[*Exeunt.*

END of the SECOND ACT.

ACT

ACT III.

Miss GRANTAM *and Miss* GODFREY.

Miss Godfrey.

UPON my word, Miss Grantam, this is but an idle piece of curiosity : you know the man is already dispos'd of, and therefore——

M. Gr. That is true, my dear ; but there is in this affair some mystery that I must and will have explain'd.

M. God. Come, come, I know the grievance. You can't brook that this spark, though even a married man, should throw off his allegiance to you, and enter a volunteer in my service.

M. Gr. And so you take this fact for granted?

M. God. Have I not his letter?

M. Gr. Conceited creature !—I fancy, Miss, by your vast affection for this letter, it is the first of the kind you ever receiv'd.

M. God. Nay, my dear, why should you be piqu'd at me ? the fault is none of mine; I dropt no handkerchief ; I threw out no lure : the bird came willing to hand, you know.

M. Gr. Metaphorical too ! what, you are setting up for a wit as well as a belle ! why really, Madam, to do you justice, you have full as fine pretentions to one as the other.

M. God. I fancy, Madam, the world will not form their judgment of either from the report of a disappointed rival.

M. Gr.

M. Gr. Rival! admirably rally'd!—But, let me tell you, Madam, this fort of behaviour, Madam, at your own houfe, whatever may be your beauty, is no great proof of your breeding, Madam.

M. God. As to that, Ma'am, I hope I fhall always fhew a proper refentment to any infult that is offer'd me, let it be in whofe houfe it will. The affignation, Ma'am, both time and place, was of your own contriving.

M. Gr. Mighty well, Ma'am!

M. God. But if, dreading a mortification, you think proper to alter your plan, your chair, I believe, is in waiting.

M. Gr. It is, Madam! then let it wait—Oh, what that was your fcheme! but it won't take, Mifs: the contrivance is a little too fhallow.

M. God. I don't underftand you.

M. Gr. Cunning creature! So all this infolence was concerted, it feems; a plot to drive me out of the houfe, that you might have the fellow all to yourfelf: but I have a regard for your character, though you negleft it. Fie, Mifs! a paffion for a married man! I really blufh for you.

M. God. And I moft fincerely pity you. But curb your choler a little: the enquiry you are about to make requires rather a cooler difpofition of mind; and by this time the hero is at hand.

M. Gr. Mighty well; I am prepar'd. But, Mifs Godfrey, if you really wifh to be acquitted of all artificial underhand dealings, in this affair, fuffer me in your name to manage the interview.

M. God. Moft willingly. But he will recolleft your voice.

M. Gr.

M. Gr. Oh, that is eafily alter'd. [*Enter a Maid, who whifpers Mifs* Grantam, *and exit.*] It is he, but hide yourfelf, Mifs, if you pleafe.

M. God. Your hood a little forwarder, Mifs: you may be known, and then we fhall have the language of politenefs inflam'd to proofs of a violent paffion.

M. Gr. You are prodigioufly cautious.

Enter YOUNG WILDING.

Y. Wild. This rendezvous is fomething in the Spanifh tafte, imported, I fuppofe, with the guittar. At prefent, I prefume, the cuftom is confin'd to the great; but it will defcend, and in a couple of months I fhall not be furpriz'd to hear an attorney's hackney clerk roufing at midnight, a millener's 'prentice, with an " Ally, Ally Croker." But that, if I miftake not, is the temple; and fee my goddefs herfelf. Mifs Godfrey!

M. Gr. Hufh.

Y. Wild. Am I right, Mifs?

M. Gr. Softly. You receiv'd my letter, I fee, Sir.

Y. Wild. And flew to the appointment with more——

M. Gr. No raptures, I beg. But you muft not fuppofe this meeting meant to encourage your hopes.

Y. Wild. How, Madam!

M. Gr. Oh, by no means, Sir; for tho' I own your figure is pleafing, and your converfation—

M. God. Hold, Mifs; when did I ever converfe with him?

M. Gr. Why, did not you fee him in the Park?

M. God.

M. God. True, Madam: but the converſation was with you.

M. Gr. Bleſs me! you are very difficult, I ſay, Sir, though your perſon may be unexceptionable, yet your character——

Y. Wild. My character!

M. Gr. Come, come, you are better known than you imagine.

Y. Wild. I hope not.

M. Gr. Your name is Wilding.

Y. Wild. How the deuce came ſhe by that! Trueˆ, Madam.

M. Gr. Pray have you never heard of Miſs Grantam?

Y. Wild. Frequently.

M. Gr. You have. And had you never any favourable thoughts of that lady? Now mind, Miſs.

Y. Wild. If you mean as a lover, never. The lady did me the honour to have a ſmall deſign upon me.

M. God. I hear every word, Miſs.

M. Gr. But you need not lean ſo heavy upon me; he ſpeaks loud enough to be heard.——I have been told, Sir, that——

Y. Wild. Yes, Ma'am, and very likely by the lady herſelf.

M. Gr. Sir!

Y. Wild. Oh, Madam, I have another obligation in my pocket to Miſs Grantam, which muſt be diſcharg'd in the morning.

M. Gr. Of what kind?

Y. Wild. Why the lady, finding an old humble ſervant of her's a little lethargic, has thought fit to adminiſter me in a jealous draught, in order to quicken his paſſion.

M. Gr. Sir, let me tell you——

M. God.

THE LYAR.

M. God. Have a care; you will betray yourself.

Y. Wild. Oh, the whole ſtory will afford you infinite diverſion: ſuch a farago of fights and feaſts. But, upon my honour, the girl has a fertile invention.

M. God. So! what that ſtory was your's was it?

Y. Wild. Pray, Madam, don't I hear another voice?

M. Gr. A diſtant relation of mine.——Every ſyllable falſe.—But, Sir, we have another charge againſt you. Do you know any thing of a lady at Abington?

Y. Wild. Miſs Grantam again. Yes, Madam, I have ſome knowledge of that lady.

M. Gr. You have! Well, Sir, and that being the caſe, how could you have the aſſurance——

Y. Wild. A moment's patience, Ma'am. That lady, that Berkſkire lady, will, I can aſſure you, prove no bar to my hopes.

M. Gr. How, Sir, no bar?

Y. Wild: Not in the leaſt, Ma'am; for that lady exiſts in idea only.

M. Gr. No ſuch perſon!

Y. Wild. A meer creature of the imagination.

M. Gr. Indeed?

Y. Wild. The attacks of Miſs Grantam were ſo powerfully enforc'd too by paternal athority, that I had no method of avoiding the blow, but by ſheltering myſelf under the conjugal ſhield.

M. Gr. You are not marry'd then?—But what credit can I give to the profeſſions of a man, who, in an article of ſuch importance, and to a perſon of ſuch reſpect——

Y. Wild,

Y. Wild. Nay, Madam, furely Mifs Godfrey fhould not accufe me of a crime her own charms have occafion'd. Could any other motive but the fear of lofing her prevail on me to trifle with a father, or compel me to infringe thofe laws which I have hitherto fo invariably obferv'd?

M. Gr. What laws, Sir?

Y. Wild. The facred laws of truth, Ma'am.

M. Gr. There, indeed you did yourfelf an infinite violence. But when the whole of the affair is difcover'd, will it be fo eafy to get rid of Mifs Grantam? the violence of her paffion, and the old gentleman's obftinacy——

Y. Wild. Are nothing to a mind refolv'd.

M. Gr. Poor Mifs Grantam!

Y. Wild. Do you know her, Madam?

M. Gr. I have heard of her: but you, Sir, I fuppofe, have been long on an intimate footing?

Y. Wild. Bred up together from children.

M. Gr. Brave!—Is fhe handfome?

Y. Wild. Her paint comes from Paris, and her femme de chambre is an excellent artift.

M. Gr. Very well—Her fhape?

Y. Wild. Pray, Madam, is not Curzon efteemed the beft ftay-maker for people inclin'd to be crooked?

M. Gr. But as to the qualities of her mind: for inftance her underftanding?

Y. Wild. Uncultivated.

M. Gr. Her wit?

Y. Wild. Borrow'd.

M. Gr. Her tafte?

Y. Wild. Trifling?

M. Gr. And her temper.?

Y. Wild. Intolerable.

M. Gr. A finish'd picture. But come these are not your real thoughts; this is a sacrifice you think due to the vanity of our sex.

Y. Wild. My honest sentiments: and to convince you how thoroughly indifferent I am to that lady, I would, upon my veracity, as soon take a wife from the grand signior's seraglio.— Now, Ma'am, I hope you are satisfy'd

M. Gr. And you would not scruple to acknowledge this before the lady's face?

Y. Wild. The first opportunity.

M. Gr. That I will take care to provide you. Dare you meet me at her house?

Y. Wild. When?

M. Gr. In half an hour.

Y. Wild. But won't a declaration of this sort appear odd at——a——

M. Gr. Come, no evasion; your conduct and character seem to me a little equivocal, and I must insist on this proof, at least of——

Y. Wild. You shall have it.

M. Gr. In half an hour.

Y. Wild. This instant.

M. Gr. Be punctual.

Y. Wild. Or may I forfeit your favour.

M. Gr. Very well: till then, Sir, adieu.—— Now I think I have my spark in the toil; and if the fellow has any feeling, if I don't make him smart for every article——Come, my dear, I shall stand in need of your aid. [*Exeunt.*

Y. Wild. So! I am now, I think, arriv'd at a critical period. If I can but weather this point ——But why should I doubt it? it is in the day of distress only that a great man displays his abilities. But I shall want Papillion: where can the puppy be?

Enter

Enter Papillion.

Y. Wild. So, Sir; where have you been rambling?

Pap. I did not suppose you would want——

Y. Wild. Want!—you are always out of the way: Here have I been forc'd to tell forty lies upon my own credit, and not a single soul to vouch for the truth of them.

Pap. Lord, Sir, you know——

Y. Wild. Don't plague me with your apologies; but it is lucky for you that I want your assistance. Come with me to Miss Grantam's.

Pap. On what occasion?

Y. Wild. An important one: but I'll prepare you as we walk.

Pap. Sir, I am really——I could wish you would be so good as to——

Y. Wild. What, desert your friend in the heat of battle! oh, you poltroon!

Pap. Sir, I would do any thing, but you know I have not talents

Y. Wild. I do, and for my own sake shall not task them too high.

Pap. Now I suppose the hour is come when we shall pay for all.

Y. Wild. Why, what a dastardly, hen-hearted ——But come, Papillion, this shall be your last campaign. Don't droop, man; confide in your leader, and remember, Sub auspice Teucro nil desperandum. [*Exeunt.*

SCENE a Room.

Enter a SERVANT, *conducting in* OLD WILDING.

Serv. My lady, Sir, will be at home immediately. Sir James Elliot is in the next room waiting her return.

O. Wild. Pray, honest friend, will you tell Sir James that I beg the favour of a word with him. [*Exit* Servant.] This unthinking boy! Half the purpose of my life has been to plan this scheme for his happiness, and in one heedless hour has he mangled all.

Enter Sir JAMES ELLIOT.

Sir, I ask your pardon: but upon so interesting a subject, I know you will excuse my intrusion. Pray, Sir, of what credit is the family of the Sybthorps in Berkshire?

Sir Ja. Sir!

O. Wild. I don't mean as to property; that I am not so solicitous about; but as to their character: Do they live in reputation? Are they respected in the neighbourhood?

Sir Ja. The family of the Sybthorps!

O. Wild. Of the Sybthorps.

O. Wild. Really I don't know, Sir.

O. Wild. Not know!

Sir Ja. No; it is the very first time I ever heard of the name.

O. Wild. How steadily he denies it! Well done, baronet! I find Jack's account was a just one. [*Aside.*] Pray, Sir James, recollect yourself.

Sir Ja.

Sir Ja. It will be to no purpofe.

O. Wild. Come, Sir, your motive for this affected ignorance is a generous, but unneceffary proof of your friendfhip for my fon: but I know the whole affair.

Sir Ja. What affair?

O. Wild. Jack's marriage.

Sir Ja. What Jack?

O. Wild. My fon Jack.

Sir Ja. Is he marry'd?

O. Wild. Is he marry'd! why you know he is.

Sir. Ja. Not I, upon my honour.

O. Wild. Nay, that is going a little too far: but to remove all your fcruples at once, he has own'd it himfelf.

Sir Ja. He has.

O. Wild. Ay, ay, to me. Every circumftance; going to your new purchafe at Abington—meeting Lydia Sybthorp at the affembly—their private interviews—furpriz'd by the father—piftol—poker—and marriage; in fhort, every particular.

Sir Ja. And this account you had from your fon?

O. Wild. From Jack; not two hours ago.

Sir Ja. I wifh you joy, Sir.

O. Wild. Not much of that, I believe.

Sir Ja. Why, Sir, does the marriage difpleafe you?

O. Wild. Doubtlefs.

Sir Ja. Then I fancy you may make yourfelf eafy.

O. Wild. Why fo?

Si. Ja. You have got, Sir, the moft prudent daughter-in-law in the Britifh dominions.

O. Wild. I am happy to hear it.

Sir Ja.

Sir Ja. For though she mayn't have brought you much, I'm sure she will not cost you a farthing.

O. Wild. Ay; exactly Jack's account.

Sir Ja. She'll be easily jointur'd.

O. Wild. Justice shall be done her.

Sir Ja. No provision necessary for younger children.

O. Wild. No Sir! why not?—I can tell you, if she answers your account, not the daughter of a duke—

Sir Ja. Ha, ha, ha, ha.

O. Wild. You are very merry, Sir.

Sir Ja. What an unaccountable fellow!

O. Wild. Sir!

Sir Ja. I beg your pardon, Sir. But with regard to this marriage—

O. Wild. Well, Sir.

Sir Ja. I take the whole history to be neither more nor less than absolute fable.

O. Wild. How, Sir!

Sir Ja. Even so.

O. Wild. Why, Sir, do you think my son would dare to impose upon me?

Sir Ja. Sir, he would dare to impose upon any body. Don't I know him?

O. Wild. What do you know?

Sir Ja. I know, Sir, that his narratives gain him more applause than credit; and that, whether from constitution or habit, there is no believing a syllable he says.

O. Wild. Oh, mighty well, Sir!—He wants to turn the tables upon Jack.—But it won't do; you are forestall'd; your novels won't pass upon me.

Sir Ja. Sir!

O. Wild. Nor is the character of my son to be blasted with the breath of a bouncer.

Sir Ja.

Sir Ja. What is this?

O. Wild. No, no, Mr. Mandeville, it won't do; you are as well known here as in your own county of Hereford.

Sir Ja. Mr. Wilding, but that I am sure this extravagant behaviour owes its rise to some impudent impositions of your son, your age would scarce prove your protection.

O. Wild. Nor, Sir, but that I know my boy equal to the defence of his own honour, should he want a protector in this arm, wither'd and impotent as you may think it.

Enter Miss GRANTAM.

M. Gr. Bless me, Gentlemen, what is the meaning of this?

Sir Ja. No more, at present, Sir: I have another demand upon your son; we'll settle the whole together.

O. Wild. I am sure he will do you justice.

M. Gr. How, Sir James Elliot, I flatter'd myself that you had finish'd your visits here, Sir. Must I be the eternal object of your outrage? not only insulted in my own person, but in that of my friends! Pray, Sir, what right——

O. Wild. Madam, I ask your pardon; a disagreeable occasion brought me here: I come, Madam, to renounce all hopes of being nearer ally'd to you, my son unfortunately being marry'd already.

M. Gr. Marry'd!

Sir Ja. Yes, Madam, to a lady in the clouds; and because I have refus'd to acknowledge her family, this old gentleman has behav'd in a manner very inconsistent with his usual politeness.

H   *O. Wild.*

O. Wild. Sir, I thought this affair was to be reserv'd for another occasion; but you, it seems—

M. Gr. Oh, is that the business?—Why, I begin to be afraid we are here a little in the wrong, Mr. Wilding.

O. Wild. Madam.

M. Gr. Your son has just confirm'd Sir James Elliot's opinion, at a conference under Miss Godfrey's window.

O. Wild. Is it possible?

M. Gr. Most true; and assign'd two most whimsical motives for the unaccountable tale.

O. Wild. What can they be?

M. Gr. An aversion for me, whom he has seen but once, and an affection for Miss Godfrey, whom I am almost sure he never saw in his life.

O. Wild. You amaze me.

M. Gr. Indeed, Mr. Wilding, your son is a most extraordinary youth; he has finely perplex'd us all. I think, Sir James, you have a small obligation to him.

Sir Ja. Which I shall take care to acknowledge the first opportunity.

O. Wild. You have my consent. An abandoned profligate! was his father a proper subject for his——But I discard him.

M. Gr. Nay, now, Gentlemen, you are rather too warm: I can't think Mr. Wilding bad-hearted at the bottom. This is a levity——

O. Wild. How, Madam! a levity!

M. Gr. Take my word for it, no more; enflam'd into habit by the approbation of his juvenile friends. Will you submit his punishment to me? I think I have the means in my hands, both to satisfy your resentments, and accomplish his cure into the bargain.

Sir Ja.

THE LYAR.

Sir Ja. I have no quarrel to him, but for the ill offices he has done me with you.

M. Gr. D'ye hear, Mr. Wilding? I am afraid my opinion with Sir James muſt cement the general peace

O. Wild. Madam, I ſubmit to any—

Enter a SERVANT.

Serv. Mr. Wilding to wait upon you, Madam. [*Exit.*

M. Gr. He is punctual, I find. Come, good folks, you all act under my direction. You, Sir, will get from your ſon, by what means you think fit, the real truth of the Abington buſineſs. You muſt likewiſe ſeemingly conſent to his marriage with Miſs Godfrey, who I ſhrewdly ſuſpect he has by ſome odd accident miſtaken for me: the lady herſelf ſhall appear at your call. Come, Sir James, you will withdraw. I intend to produce another performer, who will want a little inſtruction. Kitty.

Enter KITTY.

Let John ſhew Mr. Wilding in to his father; then come to my dreſſing room: I have a ſhort ſcene to give you in ſtudy. [*Exit Kitty.*] The girl is lively, and I warrant will do her character juſtice. Come, Sir James. Nay, no ceremony: we muſt be as buſy as bees. [*Exeunt.*

O. Wild. This ſtrange boy!—But I muſt command my temper.

Y. Wild. [*ſpeaking as he enters.*] People to ſpeak with me! See what they want, Papillion.— My father here! that's unlucky enough.

O. Wild.

THE LYAR.

O. Wild. Ha, Jack! what brings you here?

Y. Wild. Why, I thought it my duty to wait upon Mifs Grantam, in order to make her fome apology for the late unfortunate——

O. Wild. Well now, that is prudently, as well as politely done.

Y. Wild. I am happy to meet, Sir, with your approbation.

O. Wild. I have been thinking, Jack, about my daughter-in-law: as the affair is public, it is not decent to let her continue longer at her father's.

Y. Wild. Sir!

O. Wild. Would it be right to fend for her home?

Y. Wild. Doubtlefs, Sir.

O. Wild. I think fo. Why then to-morrow my chariot fhall fetch her.

Y. Wild. The devil it fhall! [*Afide.*] Not quite fo foon, if you pleafe, Sir.

O. Wild. No! why not?

Y. Wild. The journey may be dangerous in her prefent condition.

O. Wild. What's the matter with her?

Y. Wild. She is big with child, Sir.

O. Wild. An audacious——Big with child! that is fortunate. But, however, an eafy carriage, and fhort ftages can't hurt her.

Y. Wild. Pardon me, Sir, I dare not truft her: fhe is fix months gone.

O. Wild. Nay, then, there may be danger indeed. But fhould I write to her father, juft to let him know that you have difcovered the fecret.

Y. Wild. By all means, Sir, it will make him extremely happy.

O. Wild.

O. Wild. Why then I will inftantly about it, pray how do you direct to him?

Y. Wild. Abington, Berkſhire.

O. Wild. True; but his addreſs?

Y. Wild. You need not trouble yourſelf, Sir: I ſhall write by this poſt to my wife, and will ſend your letter incloſ'd.

O. Wild. Ay, ay, that will do. [*Going.*

Y. Wild. So, I have parry'd that thruſt.

O. Wild. Though upon ſecond thoughts, Jack, that will rather look too familiar for an introductory letter.

Y. Wild. Sir!

O. Wild. And theſe country gentlemen are full of punctillios———No, I'll ſend him a letter apart; fo give me his direction.

Y. Wild. You have it, Sir.

O. Wild Ay, but his name: I have been ſo hurry'd that I have entirely forgot it.

Y. Wild. I am ſure ſo have I. [*Aſide.*] His name—his name, Sir—Hopkins.

O. Wild. Hopkins!

Y. Wild. Yes, Sir.

O. Wild. That is not the ſame name that you gave me before: that, if I recollect, was either Sypthorpe, or Sybthorpe.

Y. Wild. You are right, Sir: that is his paternal appellation; but the name of Hopkins he took for an eſtate of his mother's: ſo he is indiſcriminately called Hopkins or Sybthorpe; and now I recollect I have his letter in my pocket— he ſigns himſelf Sybthorpe Hopkins.

O. Wild. There is no end of this: I muſt ſtop him at once. Harkye, Sir, I think you are call'd my ſon.

Y. Wild. I hope, Sir, you have no reaſon to doubt it.

O. Wild.

O. Wild. And look upon yourſelf as a gentleman?

Y. Wild. In having the honour of deſcending from you.

O. Wild. And that you think a ſufficient pretenſion?

Y. Wild. Sir—pray, Sir—

O. Wild. And by what means do you imagine your anceſtors obtain'd that diſtinguiſhing title? By their pre-eminence in virtue, I ſuppoſe.

Y. Wild. Doubtleſs, Sir.

O. Wild. And has it never occurr'd to you, that what was gain'd by honour might be loſt by infamy?

Y. Wild. Perfectly, Sir.

O. Wild. Are you to learn what redreſs even the imputation of a lye demands, and that nothing leſs than the life of the adverſary can extinguiſh the affront.

Y. Wild. Doubtleſs, Sir.

O. Wild. Then how dare you call yourſelf a gentleman? you, whoſe whole life has been one continued ſcene of fraud and falſity! And would nothing content you but making me a partner in your infamy? not ſatisfied with violating the great band of ſociety, mutual confidence, the moſt ſacred rights of nature muſt be invaded, and your father made the innocent inſtrument to circulate your abominable impoſitions!

Y. Wild. But, Sir!

O. Wild. Within this hour my life was near ſacrific'd in defence of your fame: but perhaps that was your intention, and the ſtory of your marriage merely calculated to ſend me out of the world, as a grateful return for my bringing you into it.

Y. Wild.

THE LYAR.   63

Y. Wild. For heaven's fake, Sir.
O. Wild. What other motive?
Y. Wild. Hear me, I intreat you, Sir.
O. Wild. To be again impos'd on! no, Jack, my eyes are open'd at laft.
Y. Wild. By all that's facred, Sir——
O. Wild. I am now deaf to your delufions.
Y. Wild. But hear me, Sir, I own the Abington bufinefs——
O. Wild. An abfolute fiction?
Y. Wild. I do.
O. Wild. And how dare you——
Y. Wild. I crave but a moment's audience.
O. Wild. Go on.
Y. Wild. Previous to the communication of your intention for me, I accidently met with a lady whofe charms——
O. Wild. So! what here is another marriage trumped out: but that is a ftale device. And pray, Sir, what place does this lady inhabit? Come, come, go on; you have a fertile invention, and this is a fine opportunity. Well, Sir, and this charming lady, refiding, I fuppofe, in Nubibus——
Y. Wild. No, Sir; in London.
O. Wild. Indeed.
Y. Wild. Nay, more, and at this inftant in this houfe.
O. Wild. And her name——
Y. Wild. Godfrey,
O. Wild. The friend of Mifs Grantam?
Y. The very fame, Sir.
O. Wild. Have you fpoke to her?
Y. Wild. Parted from her not ten minutes ago, nay, am here by her appointment.
O. Wild. Has fhe favour'd your addrefs?
Y. Wild. Time, Sir, and your approbation, will, I hope.

O. Wild.

O. Wild. Lookye, Sir; as there is some little probability in this story, I shall think it worth farther enquiry. To be plain with you, I know Miss Godfrey; am intimate with her family; and though you deserve but little from me, I will endeavour to aid your intention. But if in the progress of this affair, you practise any of your usual arts; if I discover the least falshood, the least duplicity, remember you have lost a father.

Y. Wild. I shall submit without a murmur.

[*Exit* Old Wilding.

Enter PAPILLION.

Y. Wild. Well, Papillion.

Pap. Sir, here has been the devil to pay within.

Y. Wild. What's the matter?

Pap. A whole legion of cooks, confectioners, musicians, waiters, and watermen.

Y. Wild. What do they want?

Pap. You, Sir.

Y. Wild. Me!

Pap. Yes, Sir; they have brought in their bills.

Y. Wild. Bills! for what?

Pap. For the entertainment you gave last night upon the water.

Y. Wild. That I gave!

Pap. Yes, Sir; you remember the bill of fare: I am sure the very mention of it makes my mouth water

Y. Wild. Prithee are you mad? There must be some mistake; you know that I—

Pap. They have been vastly puzzled to find out your lodgings: but Mr. Robinson meeting by accident with Sir James Elliot, he was kind enough to tell him where you liv'd. Here are the bills; Almack's, twelve dozen of claret, ditto Champagne,

Champagne, Frontiniac, fweatmeats, pine-apples: the whole amount is 372l. 9s. befides mufic and fireworks.

Y. Wild. Come, Sir, this is no time for trifling.

Pap. Nay, Sir, they fay they have gone full as low as they can afford; and they were in hopes, from the great fatisfaction you exprefs'd to Sir James Elliot, that you would throw them in an additional compliment.

Y. Wild. Harkye, Mr. Papillion, if you don't ceafe your impertinence, I fhall pay you a compliment that you would gladly excufe.

Pap. Upon my faith I relate but the mere matter of fact. You know, Sir, I am but bad at invention; tho' this incident I can't help thinking is the natural fruit of your happy one.

Y. Wild. But are you ferious? is this poffible?

Pap. Moft certain. It was with difficulty I reftrain'd their impatience; but however I have difpatch'd them to your lodgings, with a promife that you fhall immediately meet them.

Y. Wild. Oh, there we fhall foon rid our hands of the troop.—Now, Papillion, I have news for you. My father has got to the bottom of the whole Abington bufinefs.

Pap. The deuce!

Y. Wild. We parted this moment. Such a fcene!!

Pap. And what was the iffue?

Y. Wild. Happy beyond my hopes. Not only an act of oblivion, but a promife to plead my caufe with the fair.

Pap. With Mifs Godfrey?

Y. Wild. Who elfe? He is now with her in another room.

Pap. And there is no—you underftand me—in all this?

I   *Y. Wild.*

Y. Wild. No, no; that is all over now—my reformation is fix'd.

Pap. As a weather-cock.

Y. Wild. Here comes my father.

Enter OLD WILDING.

O. Wild. Well, Sir, I find in this laſt article you have condeſcended to tell me the truth: the young lady is not averſe to your union; but in order to fix ſo mutable a mind, I have drawn up a ſlight contract, which you are both to ſign.

Y. Wild. With tranſport.

O. Wild. I will introduce Miſs Godfrey. [*Exit.*

Y. Wild. Did not I tell you, Papillion?

Pap. This is amazing, indeed.

Y. Wild. Am not I a happy fortunate?—But they come.

Enter OLD WILDING, *and Miſs* GODFREY.

O. Wild. If, Madam, he has not the higheſt ſenſe of the great honour you do him, I ſhall ceaſe to regard him.——There, Sir, make your own acknowledgments to that lady.

Y. Wild. Sir!

O. Wild. This is more than you merit; but let your future behaviour teſtify your gratitude.

Y. Wild. Papillion! Madam! Sir!

O. Wild. What is the puppy petrified! Why don't you go up to the lady?

Y. Wild. Up to the lady!—That lady!

O. Wild. That lady!—To be ſure. What other lady?—To Miſs Godfrey!

Y. Wild. That lady Miſs Godfrey!

O. Wild. What is all this?—Harkye, Sir: I ſee what you are at: but no trifling; I'll be no more the dupe of your double deteſtable—-Re-
collect

collect my laſt reſolution : this inſtant your hand to the contract, or tremble at the conſequence.

Y. Wild. Sir, that I hope is——might not I ——to be ſure——

O. Wild. No further evaſions! There, Sir.

Y. Wild. Heigh ho. [*Signs it.*

O. Wild. Very well. Now, Madam, your name if you pleaſe.

Y. Wild. Papillion, do you know who ſhe is?

Pap. That's a queſtion indeed! Don't you, Sir?

Y. Wild. Not I, as I hope to be ſav'd.

Enter a SERVANT.

Serv. A young lady begs to ſpeak with Mr. Wilding.

Y. Wild. With me!

M. God. A young lady with Mr. Wilding!

Serv. Seems diſtreſs'd, Madam, and extremely preſſing for admittance.

M. God. Indeed! There may be ſomething in this! You muſt permit me, Sir, to pauſe a little: who knows but a prior claim may prevent—

O. Wild How, Sir, who is this lady?

Y. Wild. It is impoſſible for me to divine, Sir.

O. Wild. You know nothing of her?

Y. Wild. How ſhould I?

O. Wild. You hear Madam.

M. God. I preſume your ſon can have no objection to the lady's appearance.

Y. Wild. Not in the leaſt, Madam.

M. God. Shew her in, John. [*Exit.*

O. Wild. No, Madam, I do'nt think there is the leaſt room for ſuſpecting him: he can't be ſo abandon'd as to——But ſhe is here. Upon my word a ſightly woman.

I 2 *Enter*

Enter KITTY *as Miss* Sybthorpe.

Kitty. Where is he?—Oh, let me throw my arms——my life—my——

Y. Wild. Heyday!

Kitty. And could you leave me? and for so long a space? Think how the tedious time has lagg'd along.

Y. Wild. Madam!

Kitty. But we are met at last, and now we will part no more.

Y. Wild. The deuce we won't!

Kitty. What, not one kind look, no tender word to hail our second meeting!

Y. Wild. What the devil is all this;

Kitty. Are all your oaths, your protestations, come to this? have I deserv'd such treatment? Quitted my father's house, left all my friends, and wander'd here alone in search of thee, thou first, last, only object of my love.

O. Wild. To what can all this tend? Harkye, Sir, unriddle this mystery.

Y. Wild. Davus, non Œdipus sum. It is beyond me, I confess. Some lunatic escap'd from her keeper, I suppose.

Kitty. Am I disown'd then, contemn'd, slighted?

O. Wild. Hold; let me enquire into this matter a little. Pray, Madam——You seem to be pretty familiar here—Do you know this gentleman?

Kitty. Too well.

O. Wild. His name?

Kitty. Wilding.

O. Wild. So far she is right. Now yours, if you please.

Kitty. Wilding.

Omnes

Omnes. Wilding!

O. Wild. And how came you by that name pray?

Kitty. Moſt lawfully, Sir: By the ſacred band, the holy tie that made us one.

O. Wild. What, marry'd to him!

Kitty. Moſt true.

Omnes. How!

Y. Wild. Sir, may I never—

O. Wild. Peace, Monſter!——One queſtion more: Your maiden name?

Kitty. Sybthorpe.

O. Wild. Lydia, from Abington, in the county of Berks?

Kitty. The ſame.

O. Wild. As I ſuſpected. So then the whole ſtory is true, and the monſter is marry'd at laſt.

Y. Wild. Me, Sir! By all that's—

O. Wild. Eternal dumbneſs ſeize the, meaſureleſs lyar!

Y. Wild. If not me, hear this gentleman—— Marquis——

Pap. Not I; I'll be drawn into none of your ſcrapes: it is a pit of your own digging, and ſo get out as well as you can. Mean time I'll ſhift for myſelf. [*Exit.*

O. Wild. What evaſion now, Monſter?

M. God. Deceiver!

O. Wild. Lyar!

M. God. Impoſtor!

Y. Wild. Why, this is a general combination to diſtract me; but I will be heard. Sir, you are groſly impos'd upon: the low contriver of this woman's ſhallow artifice I ſhall ſoon find means to diſcover: and as to you, Madam, with whom I have been ſuddenly ſurpriz'd into a contract, I moſt ſolemnly declare this is the firſt time I ever ſat eyes on you.

O. Wild.

O. Wild. Amazing confidence! Did not bring her at your requeſt?
Y. Wild. No.
M. God. Is not this your own letter?
Y. Wild. No.
Kitty. Am not I your wife?
Y. Wild. No.
O. Wild. Did not you own it to me?
Y. Wild. Yes—that is—no, no.
Kitty. Hear me.
Y. Wild. No.
M. God. Anſwer me.
Y. Wild. No.
O. Wild. Have not I——
Y. Wild. No, no, no. Zounds you are all mad, and if I ſtay I ſhall catch the infection. [*Exit.*

Enter Sir JAMES ELLIOT *and Miſs* GRANTAM.

Omnes. Ha! ha,! ha!
M. Gr. Finely perform'd.
O. Wild. You have kept your promiſe, and I thank you, Madam.
M. Gr. My medicine was ſomewhat rough, Sir; but in deſperate caſes, you know——
O. Wild. If his cure is compleated, he will gratefully acknowledge the cauſe; if not, the puniſhment comes far ſhort of his crimes. It is needleſs to pay you any compliments, Sir James; with that Lady you can't fail to be happy. I ſhan't venture to hint a ſcheme I have greatly at heart, till we have undeniable proofs of the ſucceſs of our operations. To the ladies, indeed, no character is ſo dangerous as that of a lyar.

They in the faireſt fames can fix a flaw,
And vanquiſh females whom they never ſaw.

E P I-

EPILOGUE.

Between Miss GRANTAM and OLD WILDING.

By a Man of Fashion.

M. Gr. *HOLD, Sir.*
Our plot concluded, and strict justice done,
Let me be heard as council for your son.
Acquit I can't, I mean to mitigate :
Proscribe all lying, what would be the fate
Of this and every other earthly state ?
Consider, Sir, if once you cry it down,
You'll shut up ev'ry coffee-house in town :
The tribe of politicians will want food :
Ev'n now half famish'd---for the public good.
All Grub-street murderers of men and sense,
And every Office of intelligence,
All would be Bankrupts, the whole lying race,
And no Gazette to publish their disgrace.
　　O. Wild. *Too mild a sentence, must the good and great*
Patriots be wronged, that booksellers may eat ?
　　M. Gr. *Your patience, Sir : yet hear another word.*
Turn to the hall where justice weilds her sword:
Think in what narrow limits you would draw,
By this Proscription, all the sons of law,
For 'tis the fix'd, determin'd rule of courts,
Vyner will tell you, nay, ev'n Coke's Reports,
All pleaders may, when difficulties rise,
To gain one truth, expend a hundred lyes.
　　O. Wild. *To curb this practice I am somewhat loath :*
A lawyer has no credit but an oath.
　　　　　　　　　　　　　　　　　　M. Gr.

EPILOGUE.

M. Gr. *Then to the softer sex some favour shew:*
Leave no possession of our modest No!
O. Wild. *Oh, freely Ma'am we'll that allowance give,*
So that two Noes be held affirmative.
Provided ever that your pish and fie,
On all occasions should be deem'd a lye.
M. Gr. *Hard terms!*
On this rejoinder then I rest my cause:
Should all pay homage to Truth's sacred laws,
Let us examine what would be the case:
Why many a great man would be out of place.
O. Wild. *'Twould many a virtuous character restore.*
M. Gr. *But take a character from many more.*
O. Wild. *Tho' on the side of bad the balance fall,*
Better to find few good than fear for all.
M. Gr. *Strong are your reasons: yet, ere I submit,*
I mean to take the voices of the pit.
Is it your pleasures that we make a rule,
That ev'ry liar be proclaim'd a fool,
Fit subjects for our author's ridicule?

F I N I S.

THE

PATRON:

A

COMEDY

IN THREE ACTS.

As performed at the

THEATRE in the HAY-MARKET.

WRITTEN BY

SAMUEL FOOTE, Efq;

THE FOURTH EDITION.

LONDON:
Printed for T. LOWNDES, No. 77, Fleet-Street.
M DCC LXXXI.
[Price One Shilling and Sixpence.]

TO THE RIGHT HONOURABLE

Granville Levefon Gower,

EARL GOWER,

Lord Chamberlain of his Majefty's Houfhold.

My Lord,

THE following little comedy, founded on a ftory of M. Marmontelle's, and calculated to expofe the frivolity and ignorance of the pretenders to learning, with the infolence and vanity of their fuperficial, illiberal protectors, can be addreffed to no nobleman with more propriety than to Lord Gower; whofe judgment, though elegant, is void of affectation; and whofe patronage, though powerful, is deftitute of all faftidious parade. It is with pleafure, my Lord, that the Public fees your Lordfhip plac'd at the head of that department which is to decide, without appeal,

DEDICATION.

on the moſt popular domain in the whole republic of letters; a ſpot that has always been diſtinguiſhed with affection, and cultivated with care, by every ruler the leaſt attentive to either chaſtiſing the morals, poliſhing the manners, or, what is of equal importance, rationally amuſing the leiſure of the people.

The Patron, my Lord, who now begs your protection, has had the good fortune to be well receiv'd by the public; and, indeed, of all the pieces that I have had the honour to offer them, this ſeems to me to have the faireſt claim to their favour.

But the play, ſtripp'd of thoſe theatrical ornaments for which it is indebted to your Lordſhip's indulgence, muſt now plead it's own cauſe; nor will I, my Lord, with an affected humility, echo the trite, coarſe, though claſſical compliment, of *Optimus patronus, peſſimus poeta:* for if this be really true of the laſt, the firſt can have but ſmall pretenſions to praiſe; patronizing bad poets being, in my poor opinion, full as pernicious to the progreſs of letters, as neglecting the good.

In

DEDICATION.

In humble hopes, then, my Lord, of not being thought the meaneſt in the Muſes train, I have taken the liberty to prefix your name to this dedication, and publickly to acknowledge my obligations to your Lordſhip; which, let mê boaſt too, I have had the happineſs to receive, untainted by the inſolence of domeſtics, the delays of office, or the chilling ſuperiority of rank; mortifications which have been too often experienced by much greater writers than myſelf, from much leſs men than your Lordſhip.

My Lord, I have the honour to be, with the greateſt reſpect and gratitude,

Your Lordſhip's moſt oblig'd,

and moſt devoted,

humble ſervant,

Weſt-End,
June 20, 1764.   SAMUEL FOOTE.

Dramatis Personæ.

Sir THOMAS LOFTY, } Mr. FOOTE.
Sir PETER PEPPERPOT, }
DICK BEVER,   Mr. DEATH.
FRANK YOUNGER,   Mr. DAVIS.
Sir ROGER DOWLAS,   Mr. PALMER.
Mr. RUST,   Mr. WESTON.
Mr. DACTYL,   Mr. GRANGER.
Mr. PUFF,   Mr. HAYES.
Mr. STAYTAPE,   Mr. BROWN.
ROBIN,   Mr. PARSONS.
JOHN,   Mr. LEWIS.
Two Blacks.
Miss JULIET,   Mrs. GRANGER.

THE
PATRON.

ACT I.

Scene the Street.

Enter BEVER *and* YOUNGER.

YOUNGER.

O, Dick, you muſt pardon me.

BEVER.

Nay, but to ſatisfy your curioſity.

YOUNGER.

I tell you, I have not a jot.

BEVER.

Why then to gratify me.

YOUNGER

YOUNGER.
At rather too great an expence.

BEVER.
To a fellow of 'your obfervation and turn, I fhould think now˙ fuch a fcene a moſt delicate treat.

YOUNGER.
Delicate! Palling, naufeous, to a dreadful degree. To a lover, indeed, the charms of the niece may palliate the uncle's fulfome formality.

BEVER.
The uncle! ay, but then you know he is only one of the group.

YOUNGER.
That's true; but the figures are all finiſh'd alike:—a *maniere*, a tirefome famenefs throughout.

BEVER.
There you will excufe me; I am fure there is no want of variety.

YOUNGER.
No! then let us have a detail. Come, Dick, give us a bill of the play.

BEVER.
Firſt, you know, there's Juliet's uncle.

YOUNGER.
What, Sir Thomas Lofty! the modern Midas, or rather (as fifty dedications will tell

tell you) the Pollio, the Atticus, the patron of genius, the protector of arts, the paragon of poets, decider on merit, chief justice of taste, and sworn appraiser to Apollo and the tuneful Nine. Ha, ha.--Oh, the tedious, insipid, insufferable coxcomb!

BEVER.

Nay, now, Frank, you are too extravagant. He is universally allow'd to have taste; sharp-judging Adriel, the muse's friend, himself a muse.

YOUNGER.

Taste! by who? underling bards, that he feeds; and broken booksellers, that he bribes. Look ye, Dick, what raptures you please, when Miss Lofty is your theme; but expect no quarter for the rest of the family. I tell thee once for all, Lofty is a rank impostor, the bufo of an illiberal, mercenary tribe; he has neither genius to create, judgment to distinguish, or generosity to reward; his wealth has gain'd him flattery from the indigent, and the haughty insolence of his pretence, admiration from the ignorant. *Voilà le portrait de votre oncle.* Now on to the next.

BEVER.

The ingenious and erudite Mr. Rust.

YOUNGER.

YOUNGER.

What, old Martin, the medal-monger?

BEVER.

The fame, and my rival in Juliet.

YOUNGER.

Rival! what, Ruft? why fhe's too modern for him by a couple of centuries. Martin! why he likes no heads but upon coins. Marry'd! the mummy! Why 'tis not above a fortnight ago that I faw him making love to the figure without a nofe in Somerfet-Gardens: I caught him ftroaking the marble plaits of her gown, and afked him if he was not afhamed to take fuch liberties with ladies in public.

BEVER.

What an inconftant old fcoundrel it is!

YOUNGER.

Oh, a Dorimant. But how came this about? what could occafion the change? was it in the power of flefh and blood to feduce this adorer of virtù from his marble and porphyry?

BEVER.

Juliet has done it; and, what will furprize you, his tafte was a bawd to the bufinefs.

YOUNGER.

THE PATRON.

YOUNGER.

Prythee explain.

BEVER.

Juliet met him laſt week at her uncle's: he was a little pleaſed with the Greek of her profile; but, on a cloſer enquiry, he found the turn-up of her noſe to exactly reſemble the buſt of the princeſs Popæa.

YOUNGER.

The chaſte moiety of the amiable Nero.

BEVER.

The ſame.

YOUNGER.

Oh, the deuce! then your buſineſs was done in an inſtant.

BEVER.

Immediately. In favour of the tip, he offered *carte blanche* for the reſt of the figure, which (as you may ſuppoſe) was inſtantly caught at.

YOUNGER.

Doubtleſs. But who have we here?

BEVER.

This is one of Lofty's companions, a Weſt-Indian of an over-grown fortune. He ſaves me the trouble of a portrait. This is Sir Peter Pepperpot.

Enter

THE PATRON.

Enter Sir PETER PEPPERPOT *and two blacks.*

Sir PETER.

Carelefs fcoundrels! harkee, rafcals! I'll banifh you home, you dogs! you fhall back, and broil in the fun. Mr. Bever, your humble; Sir, I am your entirely devoted.

BEVER.

You feem mov'd; what has been the matter, Sir Peter?

Sir PETER.

Matter! why I am invited to dinner on a barbicu, and the villains have forgot my bottle of chian.

YOUNGER.

Unpardonable.

Sir PETER.

Ay, this country has fpoil'd them; this fame chriftening will ruin the colonies.------ Well, dear Bever, rare news, boy; our fleet is arriv'd from the Weft.

BEVER.

It is?

Sir PETER.

Ay, lad; and a glorious cargo of turtle. It was lucky I went to Brighthelm-ftone; I nick'd the time to a hair; thin as a lath, a lath, and a ſtomach as ſharp as a ſhark's: never was in finer condition for feeding.

BEVER.

Have you a large importation, Sir Peter?

Sir PETER.

Nine; but ſeven in excellent order: the captain aſſures me they greatly gain'd ground on the voyage.

BEVER.

How do you diſpoſe of them?

Sir PETER.

Four to Cornhill, three to Almack's, and the two ſickly ones I ſhall ſend to my borough in Yorkſhire.

YOUNGER.

Ay! what, have the provincials a reliſh for turtle?

Sir PETER.

Sir, it is amazing how this country improves in turtle and turnpikes; to which (give me leave to ſay) we, from our part of the world, have not a little contributed. Why formerly, Sir, a brace of bucks on the mayor's annual day was thought a pretty moderate bleſſing. But we, Sir, have poliſh'd their palates. Why, Sir, not the meaneſt member of my corporation but can diſtinguiſh the paſh from the pee.

YOUNGER.

YOUNGER.

Indeed!

Sir PETER.

Ay, and fever the green from the shell, with the skill of the ablest anatomist.

YOUNGER.

And they are fond of it?

Sir PETER.

Oh, that the consumption will tell you. The stated allowance is six pounds to an alderman, and five to each of their wives.

BEVER.

A plentiful provision.

Sir PETER.

But there was never known any waste: the mayor, recorder, and rector, are permitted to eat as much as they please.

YOUNGER.

The entertainment is pretty expensive.

Sir PETER.

Land-carriage and all. But I contriv'd to smuggle the last that I sent them.

BEVER.

Smuggle! I don't understand you.

Sir PETER.

Why, Sir, the rascally coachman had always charged me five pounds for the carriage. Damn'd dear! Now my cook going

ing at the fame time into the country, I made him clap a capuchin upon the turtle, and for thirty fhillings put him an infide paffenger in the Doncafter Fly.

YOUNGER.

A happy expedient.

BEVER.

Oh, Sir Peter has infinite humour.

Sir PETER.

Yes, but the frolick had like to have prov'd fatal.

YOUNGER.

How fo?

Sir PETER.

The maid at the Rummer at Hatfield popp'd her head into the coach to know if the company would have any breakfaft: Ecod, the turtle, Sir, laid hold of her nofe, and flapp'd her face with his fins, till the poor devil fell into a fit. Ha, ha, ha.

YOUNGER.

Oh, an abfolute Rabelais.

BEVER.

What, I reckon, Sir Peter, you are going to the Square?

Sir PETER.

Yes; I extremely admire Sir Thomas. You know this is his day of affembly; I
fuppofe

suppose you will be there: I can tell you, you are a wonderful favourite.

BEVER.

Am I?

Sir PETER.

He says, your natural genius is fine; and, when polish'd by his cultivation, will surprize and astonish the world.

BEVER.

I hope, Sir, I shall have your voice with the public.

Sir PETER.

Mine! O fye, Mr. Bever.

BEVER.

Come, come, you are no inconsiderable patron.

Sir PETER.

He, he, he. Can't say but I love to encourage the arts.

BEVER.

And have contributed largely yourself.

YOUNGER.

What, is Sir Peter an author?

Sir PETER.

O fye! what me? a mere dabbler; have blotted my fingers, 'tis true:—some sonnets, that have not been thought wanting in salt.

BEVER.

And your epigrams.

Sir PETER.
Not entirely without point.

BEVER.
But come, Sir Peter, the love of the arts is not the sole cause of your visits to the house you are going to.

Sir PETER.
I don't understand you.

BEVER.
Miss Juliet, the niece.

Sir PETER.
O fye! what chance have I there? Indeed, if Lady Pepperpot should happen to pop off—

BEVER.
I don't know that. You are, Sir Peter, a dangerous man; and, were I a father, or uncle, I should not be a little shy of your visits.

Sir PETER.
Psha! dear Bever, you banter.

BEVER.
And (unless I am extremely out in my guess) that lady—

Sir PETER.
Hey! what, what, dear Bever?

BEVER.
But if you should betray me—

Sir PETER.

May I never eat a bit of green fat, if I do!

BEVER.

Hints have been dropp'd.

Sir PETER.

The devil! come a little this way.

BEVER.

Well made; not robuft and gigantic, 'tis true, but extremely genteel.

Sir PETER.

Indeed!

BEVER.

Features, not entirely regular; but marking, with an air now, fuperior; greatly above the--- you underftand me?

Sir PETER.

Perfectly. Something noble; expreffive of---fafhion.

BEVER.

Right.

Sir PETER.

Yes, I have been frequently told fo.

BEVER.

Not an abfolute wit; but fomething infinitely better: an *enjouement*, a fpirit, a---

Sir PETER.

Gaiety. I was ever fo, from a child.

BEVER.

BEVER.

In short, your dress, address, with a thousand other particulars that at present I can't recollect.

Sir PETER.

Why, dear Bever, to tell thee the truth, I have always admir'd Miss Juliet, and a delicate creature she is: sweet as a sugar-cane, strait as a bamboo, and her teeth as white as a negro's.

BEVER.

Poetic, but true. Now only conceive, Sir Peter, such a plantation of perfections to be devoured by that caterpillar Rust.

Sir PETER.

A liquorish grub! Are pine-apples for such muckworms as he? I'll send him a jar of citrons and ginger, and poison the pipkin.

BEVER.

No, no.

Sir PETER.

Or invite him to dinner, and mix rat's-bane along with his curry.

BEVER.

Not so precipitate; I think we may defeat him without any danger.

Sir PETER.

How, how?

BEVER,

BEVER.

I have a thought---but we muſt ſettle the plan with the lady. Could not you give her the hint, that I ſhould be glad to ſee her a moment.

Sir PETER.

I'll do it directly.

BEVER.

But don't let Sir Thomas perceive you.

Sir PETER.

Never fear. You'll follow?

BEVER.

The inſtant I have ſettled matters with her; but fix the old fellow ſo that ſhe may not be miſs'd.

Sir PETER.

I'll nail him, I warrant; I have his opinion to beg on this manuſcript.

BEVER.

Your own?

Sir PETER.

No.

BEVER.

Oh ho! what ſomething new from the doctor, your chaplain?

Sir PETER.

He! no, no. O Lord, he's elop'd.

Beaver

THE PATRON.

BEVER.

How!

Sir PETER.

Gone. You know he was to dedicate his volume of fables to me: fo I gave him thirty pounds to get my arms engrav'd, to prefix (by way of print) to the frontifpiece; and, O grief of griefs! the doctor has mov'd off with the money. I'll fend you Mifs Juliet. [*Exit*.

BEVER.

There now is a fpecial protector! The arts, I think, can't but flourifh under fuch a Mecænas.

YOUNGER.

Heaven vifits with a tafte the wealthy fool.

BEVER.

True; but then, to juftify the difpenfation,

From hence the poor are cloath'd, the hungry fed, Fortunes to bookfellers, to authors bread.

YOUNGER.

The diftribution is, I own, a little unequal: and here comes a moft melancholy inftance; poor Dick Dactyl, and his publifher Puff.

Enter

Enter DACTYL *and* PUFF.

PUFF.

Why, then, Mr. Dactyl, carry them to somebody else; there are people enough in the trade: but I wonder you would meddle with poetry; you know it rarely pays for the paper.

DACTYL.

And how can one help it, Mr. Puff? Genius impels, and when a man is once lifted in the service of the Muses---

PUFF.

Why, let him give them warning as soon as he can. A pretty sort of service, indeed! where there are neither wages nor vails. The Muses! And what, I suppose this is the livery they give. Gadzooks, I had rather be a waiter at Ranelagh.

BEVER.

The poet and publisher at variance! What is the matter, Mr. Dactyl?

DACTYL.

As Gad shall judge me, Mr. Bever, as pretty a poem, and so polite; not a mortal can take any offence; all full of panegyric and praise.

PUFF.

PUFF.

A fine character he gives of his works. No offence! the greatest in the world, Mr. Dactyl. Panegyric and praise! and what will that do with the publick? Why who the devil will give money to be told that Mr. Such-a-one is a wiser or better man than himself? No, no; 'tis quite and clean out of nature. A good sousing satire now, well powder'd with personal pepper, and season'd with the spirit of party; that demolishes a conspicuous character, and sinks him below our own level; there, there, we are pleas'd; there we chuckle, and grin, and tofs the half-crowns on the counter.

DACTYL.

Yes, and so get cropp'd for a libel.

PUFF.

Cropp'd! ay, and the luckiest thing that can happen to you. Why, I would not give two-pence for an author that is afraid of his ears. Writing, writing is, (as I may say,) Mr. Dactyl, a sort of a warfare, where none can be victor that is the least afraid of a scar. Why, zooks, Sir, I never got salt to my porridge till I mounted at the Royal Exchange.

BEVER.

THE PATRON.

BEVER.

Indeed!

PUFF.

No, no; that was the making of me. Then my name made a noise in the world. Talk of forked hills, and of Helicon! romantic and fabulous stuff. The true Castalian stream is a shower of eggs, and a pillory the poet's Parnassus.

DACTYL.

Ay, to you indeed it may answer; but what do we get for our pains?

PUFF.

Why, what the deuce would you get? food, fire, and fame. Why you would not grow fat! a corpulent poet is a monster, a prodigy! No, no; spare diet is a spur to the fancy; high feeding would but founder your Pegasus.

DACTYL.

Why, you impudent, illiterate rascal! who is it you dare treat in this manner?

PUFF.

Heyday! what is the matter now?

DACTYL.

And is this the return for all the obligations you owe me? But no matter? the world,

world, the world shall know what you are, and how you have us'd me.

PUFF.

Do your worst; I despise you.

DACTYL.

They shall be told from what a dunghill you sprang. Gentlemen, if there be faith in a sinner, that fellow owes every shilling to me.

PUFF.

To thee!

DACTYL.

Ay, Sirrah, to me. In what kind of way did I find you? then where and what was your state? Gentlemen, his shop was a shed in Moorfields; his kitchen, a broken pipkin of charcoal; and his bed-chamber, under the counter.

PUFF.

I never was fond of expence; I ever minded my trade.

DACTYL.

Your trade! and pray with what stock did you trade? I can give you the catalogue; I believe it won't overburthen my memory. Two odd volumes of Swift; the Life of Moll Flanders, with cuts; the Five Senses, printed and coloured by Overton;
a few

a few claffics, thumb'd and blotted by the boys of the Charterhoufe; with the Trial of Dr. Sacheveral.

PUFF.

Malice.

DACTYL.

Then, Sirrah, I gave you my Canning: it was fhe firft fet you afloat.

PUFF.

A grub.

DACTYL.

And it is not only my writings: you know, Sirrah, what you owe to my phyfick.

BEVER.

How! a phyfician?

DACTYL.

Yes, Mr. Bever; phyfick and poetry. Apollo is the patron of both: *Opiferque per orbem dicor.*

PUFF.

His phyfick!

DACTYL.

My phyfick! ay, my phyfick: why, dare you deny it, you rafcal! What, have you forgot my powders for flatulent crudities?

PUFF.

No.

DAC-

DACTYL.

My cofmetic lozenge, and fugar-plumbs?

PUFF.

No.

DACTYL.

My coral for cutting of teeth, my potions, my lotions, my pregnancy-drops, with my pafte for fuperfluous hairs?

PUFF.

No, no; have you done?

DACTYL.

No, no, no; but I believe this will fuffice for the prefent.

PUFF.

Now would not any mortal believe that I ow'd my all to this fellow.

BEVER.

Why, indeed, Mr. Puff, the balance does feem in his favour.

PUFF.

In his favour! why you don't give any credit to him: a reptile, a bug, that owes his very being to me.

DACTYL.

I, I, I!

PUFF.

You, you! What, I fuppofe, you forget your garret in Wine-office-court, when you
furnifh'd

furnish'd paragraphs for the Farthing-post at twelve-pence a dozen.

DACTYL.

Fiction.

PUFF.

Then, did not I get you made collector of casualties to the Whitehall and St. James's? but that post your laziness lost you. Gentlemen, he never brought them a robbery till the highwayman was going to be hang'd; a birth till the christening was over; nor a death till the hatchment was up.

DACTYL.

Mighty well!

PUFF.

And now, because the fellow has got a little in flesh, by being puff to the playhouse this winter, (to which, by the bye, I got him appointed,) he is as proud and as vain as Voltaire. But I shall soon have him under; the vacation will come.

DACTYL.

Let it.

PUFF.

Then I shall have him sneaking and cringing, hanging about me, and begging a bit of translation.

DACTYL.

I beg, I, for tranflation!

PUFF.

No, no, not a line; not if you would do it for two-pence a fheet. No boil'd beef and carrot at mornings; no more cold pudding and porter. You may take your leave of my fhop.

DACTYL.

Your fhop! then at parting I will leave you a legacy.

BEVER.

O fye, Mr. Dactyl!

PUFF.

Let him alone.

DACTYL.

Pray, gentlemen, let me do myfelf juftice.

BEVER.

Younger, reftrain the publifher's fire.

YOUNGER.

Fye, gentlemen, fuch an illiberal combat—it is a fcandal to the republic of letters.

BEVER.

Mr. Dactyl, an old man, a mechanic, beneath—

DAC-

DACTYL.

Sir, I am calm; that thought has reſtor'd me. To your inſignificancy you are indebted for ſafety. But what my generoſity has ſaved, my pen ſhall deſtroy.

PUFF.

Then you muſt get ſomebody to mend it.

DACTYL.

Adieu!

PUFF.

Farewel! [*Exeunt ſeverally.*

BEVER.

Ha, ha, ha! come, let us along to the ſquare.
Blockheads with reaſon wicked wits abhor,
But dunce with dunce is barb'rous civil war.

END of the FIRST ACT.

ACT.

ACT II. *Scene continues.*

Enter BEVER *and* YOUNGER.

YOUNGER.

POOR Dactyl! and dwells such mighty rage in little men? I hope there is no danger of bloodshed.

BEVER.

Oh; not in the least: the *gens vatum*, the nation of poets, though an irritable, are yet a placable people. Their mutual interests will soon bring them together again.

YOUNGER.

But shall not we be late? The critical senate is by this time assembled.

BEVER.

I warrant you, frequent and full; where
Stately Bufo, puff'd by ev'ry quill,
Sits, like Apollo, on his forked hill.

But

But you know I muſt wait for Miſs Lofty; I am now totally directed by her. She gives me the key to all Sir Thomas's foibles, and preſcribes the moſt proper method to feed them; but what good purpoſe that will produce—

YOUNGER.

Is ſhe clever, adroit?

BEVER.

Doubtleſs. I like your aſking the queſtion of me.

YOUNGER.

Then pay an implicit obedience: the ladies, in theſe caſes, generally know what they are about. The door opens.

BEVER.

It is Juliet, and with her old Ruſt. Enter, Frank: you know the knight, ſo no introduction is wanted. [*Exit* Younger.] I ſhould be glad to hear this reverend piece of lumber make love; the courtſhip muſt certainly be curious. Good-manners, ſtand by; by your leave I will liſten a little. [Bever *retires.*]

Enter JULIET *and* RUST.

JULIET.

And your collection is large?

RUST.

RUST.

Moſt curious and capital. When, Madam, will you give me leave to add your charms to my catalogue?

JULIET.

O dear! Mr. Ruſt, I ſhall but diſgrace it. Beſides, Sir, when I marry, I am reſolv'd to have my huſband all to myſelf: now for the poſſeſſion of your heart I ſhall have too many competitors.

RUST.

How, Madam! were Prometheus alive, and would animate the Helen that ſtands in my hall, ſhe ſhould not coſt me a ſigh.

JULIET.

Ay, Sir, there lies my greateſt misfortune. Had I only thoſe who are alive to contend with, by aſſiduity, affection, cares, and careſſes, I might ſecure my conqueſt: though that would be difficult; for I am convinc'd, were you, Mr. Ruſt, put up by Preſtage to auction, the Apollo Belvidere would not draw a greater number of bidders.

RUST.

Would that were the caſe, Madam, ſo I might be thought a proper companion to the Venus de Medicis.

JULIET.

The flower of rhetoric, and pink of politeness. But my fears are not confined to the living; for every nation and age, even painters and ſtatuaries, conſpire againſt me. Nay, when the Pantheon itſelf, the very goddeſſes riſe up as my rivals, what chance has a mortal like me.——I ſhall certainly laugh in his face. [*Aſide.*]

RUST.

She is a delicate ſubject.——Goddeſſes, Madam! zooks, had you been on Mount Ida when Paris decided the conteſt, the Cyprian queen had pleaded for the pippin in vain.

JULIET.

Extravagant gallantry.

RUST.

In you, Madam, are concentered all the beauties of the Heathen mythology: the open front of Diana, the luſtre of Pallas's eyes,—

JULIET.

Oh, Sir!

RUST.

The chromatic muſick of Clio, the blooming graces of Hebè, the empereal

port

THE PATRON. 35

port of queen Juno, with the delicate dimples of Venus.

JULIET.

I fee, Sir, antiquity has not engrofs'd all your attention: you are no novice in the nature of woman. Incenfe, I own, is grateful to moft of my fex; but there are times when adoration may be difpens'd with.

RUST.

Ma'am!

JULIET.

I fay, Sir, when we women willingly wave our rank in the fkies, and wifh to be treated as mortals.

RUST.

Doubtlefs, Madam: and are you wanting in materials for that? No, Madam; as in dignity you furpafs the Heathen divinities, fo in the charms of attraction you beggar the queens of the earth. The whole world, at different periods, has contributed it's feveral beauties to form you.

JULIET.

The deuce it has! [*Afide.*]

RUST.

See there the ripe Afiatic perfection, join'd to the delicate foftnefs of Europe! In you, Madam, I burn to poffefs Cleopatra's alluring glances, the Greek profile of queen Clytemneftra, the Roman nofe of the emprefs Popæa—

JULIET.

With the majeftic march of queen Befs. Mercy on me, what a wonderful creature am I!

RUST.

In fhort, Madam, not a feature you have, but recals to my mind fome trait in a medal or buft.

JULIET.

Indeed! Why, by your account, I muft be an abfolute olio, a perfect falamongundy of charms.

RUST.

Oh, Madam, how can you demean, as I may fay, undervalue—

JULIET.

Value! there is the thing; and to tell you the truth, Mr. Ruft, in that word Value lies my greateft objection.

RUST.

I don't underftand you.

JULIET.

Why then I will explain myfelf. It has been faid, and I believe with fome fhadow

of

of truth, that no man is a hero to his *valet de chambre*: now I am afraid, when you and I grow a little more intimate, which I fuppofe muft be the cafe if you proceed on your plan, you will be horribly difappointed in your high expectations, and foon difcover this Juno, this Cleopatra, and princefs Popæa, to be as arrant a mortal as madam your mother.

RUST.

Madam, I, I, I—

JULIET.

Your patience a moment. Being therefore defirous to preferve your devotion, I beg for the future you would pleafe to adore at a diftance.

RUST.

To Endymion, Madam, Luna once liftened.

JULIET.

Ay, but he was another kind of a mortal: you may do very well as a votary; but for a hufband—mercy upon me!

RUST.

Madam, you are not in earneft, not ferious!

JULIET.

Not ferious! Why have you the impudence to think of marrying a goddefs?

RUST.

38   THE PATRON.

RUST.

I should hope—

JULIET.

And what should you hope? I find your devotion resembles that of the world: when the power of sinning is over, and the sprightly first-runnings of life are rack'd off, you offer the vapid dregs to your deity. No, no; you may, if you please, turn monk in my service. One vow, I believe, you will observe better than most of them, chastity.

RUST.

Permit me—

JULIET.

Or, if you must marry, take your Julia, your Portia, or Flora, your Fum-fam from China, or your Egyptian Osiris. You have long paid your addresses to them.

RUST.

Marry! what, marble?

JULIET.

The properest wives in the world; you can't choose amiss; they will supply you with all that you want.

RUST.

Your uncle has, Madam, consented.

JU-

JULIET.

That is more than ever his niece will. Confented! and to what? to be fwath'd to a mould'ring mummy; or be lock'd up, like your medals, to canker and ruft in a cabinet! No, no; I was made for the world, and the world fhall not be robb'd of its right.

BEVER.

Bravo, Juliet! Gad, fhe's a fine-fpirited girl.

JULIET.

My profile, indeed! No, Sir, when I marry, I muft have a man that will meet my full face.

RUST.

Might I be heard for a moment?

JULIET.

To what end? You fay, you have Sir Thomas Lofty's confent; I tell you, you can never have mine. You may fcreen me from, or expofe me to, my uncle's refentment; the choice is your own: if you lay the fault at my door, you will, doubtlefs, greatly diftrefs me; but take the blame on yourfelf, and I fhall own myfelf extremely oblig'd to you.

RUST.

How! confefs myfelf in the fault?

JULIET.

Ay; for the beſt thing a man can do, when he finds he can't be belov'd, is to take care he is not heartily hated. There is no other alternative.

RUST.

Madam, I ſha'n't break my word with Sir Thomas.

JULIET.

Nor I with myſelf. So there's an end of our conference. Sir, your very obedient.

RUST.

Madam, I, I, don't—that is, let me— But no matter. Your ſervant. [*Exit.*

JULIET.

Ha, ha, ha!

Enter BEVER *from behind.*

BEVER.

Ha, ha, ha! Incomparable Juliet! How the old dotard trembled and totter'd; he could not have been more inflam'd, had he been robb'd of his Otho.

JULIET.

Ay; was ever goddeſs ſo familiarly us'd? In my conſcience, I began to be afraid that he would treat me as the Indians do their dirty divinities; whenever they are deaf to their prayers, they beat and abuſe them.

BEVER.
But, after all, we are in an aukward fituation.

JULIET.
How fo?

BEVER.
I have my fears.

JULIET.
So have not I.

BEVER.
Your uncle has refolv'd that you fhould be marry'd to Ruft.

JULIET.
Ay, he may decree; but it is I that muft execute.

BEVER.
But fuppofe he has given his word.

JULIET.
Why then let him recal it again.

BEVER.
But are you fure you fhall have courage enough---

JULIET.
To fay No? That requires much refolution indeed.

BEVER.
Then I am at the height of my hopes.

JULIET.
Your hopes! Your hopes and your fears are ill-founded alike.

BE-

BEVER.

Why, you are determined not to be his.

JULIET.

Well, and what then?

BEVER.

What then! why then you will be mine.

JULIET.

Indeed! and is that the natural confequence? Whoever won't be his, muſt be yours. Is that the logic of Oxford?

BEVER.

Madam, I did flatter myſelf—

JULIET.

Then you did very wrong, indeed, Mr. Bever: you ſhould ever guard againſt flattering yourſelf; for of all dangerous paraſites, ſelf is the worſt.

BEVER.

I am aſtoniſh'd!

JULIET.

Aſtoniſh'd! you are mad, I believe! Why, I have not known you a month. It is true, my uncle ſays your father is his friend; your fortune, in time, will be eaſy; your figure is not remarkably faulty; and as to your underſtanding, paſſable enough for a young fellow who has not ſeen much of the world: but when one talks of a huſband---Lord, it's quite another ſort of

a---Ha,

a---Ha, ha, ha! Poor Bever, how he ſtares! he ſtands like a ſtatue!

BEVER.

Statue indeed, Madam; I am very near petrified.

JULIET.

Even then you will make as good a huſband as Ruſt. But go, run, and join the aſſembly within: be attentive to every word, motion, and look of my uncle's; be dumb when he ſpeaks, admire all he ſays, laugh when he ſmirks, bow when he ſneezes; in ſhort, fawn, flatter, and cringe; don't be afraid of over-loading his ſtomach, for the knight has a noble digeſtion, and you will find ſome there who will keep you in countenance.

BEVER.

I fly. So then, Juliet, your intention was only to try—

JULIET.

Don't plague me with impertinent queſtions: march! obey my directions. We muſt leave the iſſue to Chance; a greater friend to mankind than they are willing to own. Oh, if any thing new ſhould occur, you may come into the drawing-room for further inſtructions. [*Exeunt ſeverally.*

SCENE

THE PATRON.

SCENE a Room in Sir THOMAS LOFTY'S Houſe.

Sir THOMAS, RUST, PUFF, DACTYL, and others, diſcovered ſitting.

Sir THOMAS.

Nothing new to-day from Parnaſſus?

DACTYL.

Not that I hear.

Sir THOMAS.

Nothing critical, philoſophical, or political?

PUFF.

Nothing.

Sir THOMAS.

Then in this *diſette*, this dearth of invention, give me leave, gentlemen, to diſtribute my ſtores. I have here in my hand a little, ſmart, ſatyrical epigram; new, and prettily pointed: in ſhort, a production that Martial himſelf would not have bluſh'd to acknowledge.

RUST.

Your own, Sir Thomas?

Sir THOMAS.

O fye! no; ſent me this morning, anonymous.

DACTYL.

Pray, Sir Thomas, let us have it.

ALL.

THE PATRON.

ALL.

By all means; by all means.

Sir THOMAS.

To PHILLIS.

Think'ſt thou, fond Phillis, Strephon told thee true,
Angels are painted fair to look like you:
Another ſtory all the town will tell;
Phillis paints fair—to look like an an-gel.

ALL.

Fine! fine! very fine!

DACTYL.

Such an eaſe and ſimplicity.

PUFF.

The turn ſo unexpected and quick.

RUST.

The ſatire ſo poignant.

Sir THOMAS.

Yes; I think it poſſeſſes, in an eminent degree, the three great epigrammatical requiſites; brevity, familiarity, and ſeverity.

Phillis paints fair—to look like an an-gel.

DACTYL.

Happy! Is the Phillis, the ſubject, a ſecret?

Sir THOMAS.

Oh, dear me! nothing perſonal; no; an impromptu; a mere *jeu d'eſprit*.

PUFF.

PUFF.

Then, Sir Thomas, the secret is out; it is your own.

DACTYL.

That was obvious enough.

PUFF.

Who is there else could have wrote it?

RUST.

True, true.

Sir THOMAS.

The name of the author is needless. So it is an acquisition to the republic of letters, any gentleman may claim the merit that will.

PUFF.

What a noble contempt!

DACTYL.

What greatness of mind!

RUST.

Scipio and Lælius were the Roman Loftys. Why, I dare believe Sir Thomas has been the making of half the authors in town: he is, as I may say, the great manufacturer; the other poets are but pedlars, that live by retailing his wares.

ALL.

Ha, ha, ha! well obferv'd, Mr. Ruft.

Sir THOMAS.

Ha, ha, ha! *Molle atque facetum.* Why, to pursue the metaphor, if Sir Thomas Lofty

was

was to call in his poetical debts, I believe there would be a good many bankrupts in the Mufe's Gazette.

ALL.

Ha, ha, ha!

Sir THOMAS.

But, *à propos*, gentlemen; with regard to the eclipfe: you found my calculation exact?

DACTYL.

To a digit.

Sir THOMAS.

Total darknefs, indeed! and birds going to rooft! Thofe philomaths, thofe almanack-makers, are the moft ignorant rafcals—

PUFF.

It is amazing where Sir Thomas Lofty ftores all his knowledge.

DACTYL.

It is wonderful how the mind of man can contain it.

Sir THOMAS.

Why, to tell you the truth, that circumftance has a good deal engag'd my attention; and I believe you will admit my method of folving the phenomenon philofophical and ingenious enough.

PUFF.

Without queftion.

ALL.

ALL.

Doubtless.

Sir THOMAS.

I suppose, gentlemen, my memory, or mind, to be a chest of drawers, a kind of bureau; where, in separate cellules, my different knowledge on different subjects is stor'd.

RUST.

A prodigious discovery!

ALL.

Amazing!

Sir THOMAS.

To this cabinet volition, or will, has a key; so, when an arduous subject occurs, I unlock my bureau, pull out the particular drawer, and am supply'd with what I want in an instant.

DACTYL.

A Malbranch!

PUFF.

A Boyle!

ALL.

A Locke!

Enter SERVANT.

SERVANT.

Mr. Bever. [*Exit.*

Sir THOMAS.

A young gentleman from Oxford, recommended to my care by his father. The university

THE PATRON.

univerſity has given him a good ſolid Doric foundation; and when he has receiv'd from you a few Tuſcan touches, the Ionic and Corinthian graces, I make no doubt but he will prove a compoſite pillar to the republic of letters. [*Enter* BEVER.] This, Sir, is the ſchool from whence ſo many capital maſters have iſſued; the river that enriches the regions of ſcience.

DACTYL.

Of which river, Sir Thomas, you are the ſource: here we quaff; *et purpureo bibimus ore nectar.*

Sir THOMAS.

Purpureo! Delicate, indeed! Mr. Dactyl. Do you hear, Mr. Bever? *Bibimus ore nectar.* You, young gentleman, muſt be inſtructed to quote; nothing gives a period more ſpirit than a happy Latin quotation, nor has indeed a finer effect at the head of an eſſay. Poor Dick Steel! I have oblig'd him with many a motto for his fugitive pieces.

PUFF.

Ay, and with the contents too; or Sir Richard is fouly bely'd.

Enter SERVANT.

SERVANT.

Sir Roger Dowlas.

Sir THOMAS.

Pray defire him to enter. [*Exit* Servant.] Sir Roger, Gentlemen, is a confiderable Eaft-India proprietor; and feems defirous of collecting from this learned affembly fome rhetorical flowers, which he hopes to ftrew, with honour to himfelf, and advantage to the company, at Merchant-Taylors-Hall. [*Enter* Sir ROGER DOWLAS.] Sir Roger, be feated. This gentleman has, in common with the greateft orator the world ever faw, a fmall natural infirmity; he ftutters a little: but I have prefcrib'd the fame remedy that Demofthenes us'd, and don't defpair of a radical cure. Well, Sir, have you digefted thofe general rules?

Sir ROGER.

Pr--ett--y well, I am obli--g'd to you, Sir Thomas.

Sir THOMAS.

Have you been regular in taking your tincture of fage, to give you confidence for fpeaking in public?

Sir ROGER.

Y--es, Sir Thomas.

Sir THOMAS.

Did you open at the laft general court?

Sir ROGER.

I attem--p--ted fo--ur or fi--ve times.

Sir

Sir THOMAS.
What hinder'd your progress?

Sir ROGER.
The pe--b--bles.

Sir THOMAS.
Oh, the pebbles in his mouth. But they are only put in to practise in private; you should take them out when you are addressing the public.

Sir ROGER.
Yes; I will for the fu--ture.

Sir THOMAS.
Well, Mr. Rust, you had a *tête-à-tête* with my niece. A propos, Mr. Bever, here offers a fine occasion for you; we shall take the liberty to trouble your Muse on their nuptials. O Love! O Hymen! here prune thy purple wings; trim thy bright torch. Hey, Mr. Bever?

BEVER.
My talents are at Sir Thomas Lofty's direction; tho' I must despair of producing any performance worthy the attention of so compleat a judge of the elegant arts.

Sir THOMAS.
Too modest, good Mr. Bever. Well, Mr. Rust, any new acquisition, since our last meeting, to your matchless collection?

RUST.

RUST.

Why, Sir Thomas, I have both loft and gain'd since I saw you.

Sir THOMAS.

Loft! I am sorry for that.

RUST.

The curious sarcophagus, that was sent me from Naples by Signior Belloni—

Sir THOMAS.

You mean the urn that was suppos'd to contain the dust of Agrippa!

RUST.

Suppos'd! no doubt but it did.

Sir THOMAS.

I hope no sinister accident to that inestimable relic of Rome.

RUST.

It's gone.

Sir THOMAS.

Gone! oh, illiberal! What, stolen, I suppose, by some connoisseur?

RUST.

Worse, worse! a prey, a martyr to ignorance: a housemaid, that I hir'd last week, mistook it for a broken green chamber-pot, and sent it away in the dust-cart.

Sir THOMAS.

She merits impaling. Oh, the Hun!

DAC.

DACTYL.
The Vandal!
ALL.
The Visigoth!
RUST.
But I have this day acquir'd a treasure that will in some measure make me amends.

Sir THOMAS.
Indeed! what can that be?
PUFF.
That must be something curious, indeed.
RUST.
It has cost me infinite trouble to get it.
DACTYL.
Great rarities are not had without pains.
RUST.
It is three months ago since I got the first scent of it, and I have been ever since on the hunt; but all to no purpose.

Sir THOMAS.
I am quite upon thorns till I see it.
RUST.
And yesterday, when I had given it over, when all my hopes were grown desperate, it fell into my hands, by the most unexpected and wonderful accident.

Sir THOMAS.
Quod optanti divum promittere nemo
Auderet, volvenda dies en'attulit ultro.
Mr. Bever, you remark my quotation?

BEVER.

BEVER.

Moſt happy. Oh, Sir, nothing you ſay can be loſt.

RUST.

I have brought it here in my pocket; I am no churl; I love to pleaſure my friends.

Sir THOMAS.

You are, Mr. Ruſt, extremely obliging.

ALL.

Very kind, very obliging indeed.

RUST.

It was not much hurt by the fire.

Sir THOMAS.

Very fortunate.

RUST.

The edges are ſoil'd by the link; but many of the letters are exceedingly legible.

Sir ROGER.

A li--ttle roo--m, if you p--leaſe.

RUST.

Here it is; the precious remains of the very North-Briton that was burnt at the Royal-Exchange.

Sir THOMAS.

Number forty-five?

RUST.

The ſame.

BEVER.

You are a lucky man, Mr. Ruſt.

RUST.

THE PATRON. 55

RUST.

I think fo. But, Gentlemen, I hope I need not give you a caution : hufh—filence —no words on this matter.

DACTYL.

You may depend upon us.

RUST.

For as the paper has not fuffer'd the law, I don't know whether they may not feize it again.

Sir THOMAS.

With us you are fafe, Mr. Ruft. Well, young gentleman, you fee we cultivate all branches of fcience.

BEVER.

Amazing, indeed! But when we confider you, Sir Thomas, as the directing, the ruling planet, our wonder fubfides in an inftant. Science firft faw the day with Socrates in the Attic portico; her early years were fpent with Tully in the Tufculan fhade; but her ripe, maturer hours, fhe enjoys with Sir Thomas Lofty, near Cavendifh-Square.

Sir THOMAS.

The moft claffical compliment I ever receiv'd. Gentlemen, a philofophical repaft attends your acceptance within. Sir Roger, you'll lead the way. [*Exeunt all but* Sir Thomas *and* Bever.] Mr. Bever, may I beg your ear for a moment? Mr. Bever, the

D 4 friend-

friendship I have for your father secur'd you at first a gracious reception from me; but what I then paid to an old obligation, is now, Sir, due to your own particular merit.

BEVER.

I am happy, Sir Thomas, if—

Sir THOMAS.

Your patience. There is in you, Mr. Bever, a fire of imagination, a quickness of apprehension, a solidity of judgment, join'd to a depth of discretion, that I never yet met with in any subject at your time of life.

BEVER.

I hope I shall never forfeit—

Sir THOMAS.

I am sure you never will; and to give you a convincing proof that I think so, I am now going to trust you with the most important secret of my whole life.

BEVER.

Your confidence does me great honour.

Sir THOMAS.

But this must be on a certain condition.

BEVER.

Name it.

Sir THOMAS.

That you give me your solemn promise to comply with one request I shall make you.

BEVER.

There is nothing Sir Thomas Lofty can ask, that I shall not chearfully grant.

Sir

THE PATRON.

Sir THOMAS.

Nay, in fact it will be serving yourself.

BEVER.

I want no such inducement.

Sir THOMAS.

Enough. But we can't be too private. [*Shuts the door.*] Sit you down. Your Christian name, I think, is—

BEVER.

Richard.

Sir THOMAS.

True; the same as your father's. Come, let us be familiar. It is, I think, dear Dick, acknowledg'd, that the English have reach'd the highest pitch of perfection in every department of writing but one---the dramatic.

BEVER.

Why, the French critics are a little severe.

Sir THOMAS.

And with reason. Now, to rescue our credit, and at the same time give my country a model, [*shews a manuscript*] see here.

BEVER.

A play?

Sir THOMAS.

A *chef d'oeuvre*.

BEVER.

Your own?

Sir THOMAS.

Speak lower. I am the author.

BEVER.

BEVER.

Nay, then there can be no doubt of it's merit.

Sir THOMAS.

I think not. You will be charm'd with the fubject.

BEVER.

What is it, Sir Thomas?

Sir THOMAS.

I fhall furprize you. The ftory of Robin Crufoe. Are not you ftruck?

BEVER.

Moft prodigioufly.

Sir THOMAS.

Yes; I knew the very title would hit you. You will find the whole fable is finely conducted, and the character of Friday, *qualis ab incepto*, nobly fupported throughout.

BEVER.

A pretty difficult tafk.

Sir THOMAS.

True; that was not a bow for a boy. The piece has long been in rehearfal at Drury-lane playhoufe, and this night is to make it's appearance.

BEVER.

To-night?

Sir THOMAS.

This night.

BEVER.

I will attend, and engage all my friends to fupport it.

Sir

THE PATRON. 59

Sir THOMAS.

That is not my purpofe; the piece will want no fuch affiftance.

BEVER.

I beg pardon.

Sir THOMAS.

The manager of that houfe (who you know is a writer himfelf), finding all the anonymous things he produc'd (indeed fome of them wretched enough, and very unworthy of him) plac'd to his account by the public, is determin'd to exhibit no more without knowing the name of the author.

BEVER.

A reafonable caution.

Sir THOMAS.

Now, upon my promife (for I appear to patronize the play) to announce the author before the curtain draws up, Robinfon Crufoe is advertis'd for this evening.

BEVER.

Oh, then, you will acknowledge the piece to be your's?

Sir THOMAS.

No.

BEVER.

How then?

Sir THOMAS.

My defign is to give it to you.

BEVER.

To me!

Sir

Sir THOMAS.

To you.

BEVER.

What, me the author of Robinson Crusoe!

Sir THOMAS.

Ay.

BEVER.

Lord, Sir Thomas, it will never gain credit: so compleat a production the work of a stripling! Besides, Sir, as the merit is your's, why rob yourself of the glory?

Sir THOMAS.

I am entirely indifferent to that.

BEVER.

Then why take the trouble?

Sir THOMAS.

My fondness for letters, and love of my country. Besides, dear Dick, though the *pauci & selecti*, the chosen few, know the full value of a performance like this, yet the ignorant, the profane, (by much the majority,) will be apt to think it an occupation ill suited to my time of life.

BEVER.

Their censure is praise.

Sir THOMAS.

Doubtless. But indeed my principal motive is my friendship for you. You are now a candidate for literary honours, and I am determin'd

termin'd to fix your fame on an immoveable
basis.

BEVER.

You are most excessively kind; but there is something so disingenuous in stealing reputation from another man—

Sir THOMAS.

Idle punctilio!

BEVER.

It puts me so in mind of the daw in the fable—

Sir THOMAS.

Come, come, dear Dick, I won't suffer your modesty to murder your fame. But the company will suspect something; we will join them, and proclaim you the author. There, keep the copy; to you I consign it for ever; it shall be a secret to latest posterity. You will be smother'd with praise by our friends; they shall all in their bark to the playhouse, and there

Attendant sail,
Pursue the triumph, and partake the gale.
[*Exeunt.*

END of the SECOND ACT.

ACT.

ACT III. *Scene continues.*

Enter BEVER, *reading.*

SO ends the firſt act. Come, now for the ſecond. "Act the ſecond, ſhewing"—the coxcomb has prefac'd every act with an argument too, in humble imitation, I warrant, of Monſ. Diderot—" ſhewing the fatal effects of diſobedience to parents;" with, I ſuppoſe, the diverting ſcene of a gibbet; an entertaining ſubject for comedy. And the blockhead is as prolix—every ſcene as long as a homily. Let's ſee; how does this end? " Exit Cruſoe, and enter ſome ſavages, dancing a ſaraband." There's no bearing this abominable traſh. [*Enter* JULIET.] So, Madam; thanks to your advice and direction, I am got into a fine ſituation.

JULIET.

What is the matter now, Mr. Bever?

BEVER.

The Robinſon Cruſoe.

JU-

JULIET.
Oh, the play that is to be acted to-night. How secret you were? Who in the world would have guefs'd you was the author?
BEVER.
Me, Madam!
JULIET.
Your title is odd; but to a genius every fubject is good.
BEVER.
You are inclin'd to be pleafant:
JULIET.
Within they have been all prodigious loud in the praife of your piece; but I think my uncle rather more eager than any.
BEVER.
He has reafon; for fatherly fondnefs goes far.
JULIET.
I don't underftand you.
BEVER.
You don't!
JULIET.
No.
BEVER.
Nay, Juliet, this is too much; you know it is none of my play.
JULIET.
Whofe then?
BEVER.
Your uncle's.
JULIET.
My uncle's! then how, in the name of wonder, came you to adopt it?
BEVER.

BEVER.
At his earneſt requeſt. I may be a fool; but remember, Madam, you are the cauſe.

JULIET.
This is ſtrange; but I can't conceive what his motive could be.

BEVER.
His motive is obvious enough; to ſcreen himſelf from the infamy of being the author.

JULIET.
What, is it bad, then?

BEVER.
Bad! moſt infernal!

JULIET.
And you have conſented to own it?

BEVER.
Why, what could I do? he in a manner compell'd me.

JULIET.
I am extremely glad of it.

BEVER.
Glad of it! why, I tell you 'tis the moſt dull, tedious, melancholy—

JULIET.
So much the better.

BEVER.
The moſt flat piece of frippery that ever Grubſtreet produc'd.

JULIET.
So much the better.

BEVER.
It will be damn'd before the third act.

JULIET.

JULIET.
So much the better.

BEVER.
And I shall be hooted and pointed at wherever I go.

JULIET.
So much the better.

BEVER.
So much the better! zounds! so, I suppose, you would say if I was going to be hang'd. Do you call this a mark of your friendship?

JULIET.
Ah, Bever, Bever! you are a miserable politician. Do you know, now, that this is the luckiest incident that ever occurr'd?

BEVER.
Indeed!

JULIET.
It could not have been better laid, had we plann'd it ourselves.

BEVER.
You will pardon my want of conception: but these are riddles---

JULIET.
That at present I have not time to explain. But what makes you loit'ring here? Past six o'clock, as I live! Why, your play is begun; run, run to the house. Was ever author so little anxious for the fate of his piece?

BEVER.
My piece!

JULIET.
Sir Thomas! I know by his walk. Fly, and pray

pray all the way for the fall of your play. And, do you hear, if you find the audience too indulgent, inclin'd to be milky, rather than fail, fqueeze in a little acid yourfelf. Oh, Mr. Bever, at your return, let me fee you, before you go to my uncle; that is, if you have the good look to be damn'd.

BEVER.

You need not doubt that. [*Exit*.

Enter Sir THOMAS LOFTY.

Sir THOMAS.

So, Juliet; was not that Mr. Bever?

JULIET.

Yes, Sir.

Sir THOMAS.

He is rather tardy; by this time his caufe is come on. And how is the young gentleman affected? for this is a trying occafion.

JULIET.

He feems pretty certain, Sir.

Sir THOMAS.

Indeed I think he has very little reafon fo fear: I confefs I admire the piece; and feel a much for it's fate as if the work was my own

JULIET.

That I moft fincerely believe. I wonder, Sir, you did not choofe to be prefent.

Sir THOMAS.

Better not. My affections are ftrong, Juliet, and my nerves but tenderly ftrung; however,

intel-

intelligent people are planted, who will bring me every act a faithful account of the procefs.

JULIET.

That will anfwer your purpofe as well.

Sir THOMAS.

Indeed, I am paffionately fond of the arts, and therefore can't help---did not fomebody knock? no. My good girl, will you ftep, and take care that when any body comes the fervants may not be out of the way. [*Exit* Juliet.] Five and thirty minutes paft fix; by this time the firft act muft be over: John will be prefently here. I think it can't fail; yet there is fo much whim and caprice in the public opinion, that---This young man is unknown; they'll give him no credit. I had better have own'd it myfelf: Reputation goes a great way in thefe matters: people are afraid to find fault; they are cautious in cenfuring the works of a man who---hufh! that's he: no; 'tis only the fhutters. After all, I think I have chofe the beft way: for, if it fucceeds to the degree I expect, it will be eafy to circulate the real name of the author; if it falls, I am concealed, my fame fuffers no---There he is. [*Loud knocking.*] I can't conceive what kept him fo long. [*Enter* JOHN.] So, John; well; and---but you have been a monftrous while.

JOHN.

Sir, I was wedged fo clofe in the pit that I could fcarcely get out.

Sir THOMAS.
The houfe was full then?
JOHN.
As an egg, Sir.
Sir THOMAS.
That's right. Well John, and did matters go fwimmingly? hey?
JOHN.
Exceedingly well, Sir.
Sir THOMAS.
Exceedingly well. I don't doubt it. What, vaft clapping and roars of applaufe, I fuppofe.
JOHN.
Very well, Sir.
Sir THOMAS.
Very well, Sir! You are damn'd coftive, I think. But did not the pit and boxes thunder again?
JOHN.
I can't fay there was over-much thunder.
Sir THOMAS.
No! Oh, attentive, I reckon. Ay, attention! that is the true, folid, fubftantial applaufe. All elfe may be purchafed; hands move as they are bid: but when the audience is hufhed ftill, afraid of lofing a word, then---
JOHN.
Yes, they were very quiet indeed, Sir.
Sir THOMAS.
I like them the better, John; a ftrong mark of their great fenfibility. Did you fee Robin?
JOHN

THE PATRON. 69

JOHN.

Yes, Sir; he'll be here in a trice; I left him lift'ning at the back of the boxes, and charg'd him to make all the hafte home that he could

Sir THOMAS.

That's right, John; very well; your account pleafes me much, honeft John. [*Exit* John.] No, I did not expect the firft act would produce any prodigious effect. And, after all, the firft act is but a mere introduction; juft opens the bufinefs, the plot, and gives a little infight into the characters: fo that if you but engage and intereft the houfe, it is as much as the beft writer can flatt---[*knocking without*] Gadfo! what, Robin already! why the fellow has the feet of a Mercury. [*Enter* Robin.] Well, Robin, and what news do you bring?

ROBIN.

Sir, I, I, I,——

Sir THOMAS.

Stop, Robin, and recover your breath. Now, Robin.

ROBIN.

There has been a woundy uproar below.

Sir THOMAS.

An uproar! what, at the playhoufe?

ROBIN.

Ay.

Sir THOMAS.

At what?

ROBIN.

I don't know: belike at the words the play-folk were talking.

Sir THOMAS.

At the players! how can that be? Oh, now I begin to conceive. Poor fellow, he knows but little of plays. What, Robin, I suppose, hallowing, and clapping, and knocking of sticks?

ROBIN.

Hallowing! ay, and hooting too.

Sir THOMAS.

And hooting!

ROBIN.

Ay, and hissing to boot.

Sir THOMAS.

Hissing! you must be mistaken.

ROBIN.

By the mass, but I am not.

Sir THOMAS.

Impossible! Oh, most likely some drunken, disorderly fellows, that were disturbing the house and interrupting the play; too common a case; the people were right: they deserv'd a rebuke. Did not you hear them cry Out, out, out?

ROBIN.

Noa; that was not the cry; 'twas Off, off, off!

Sir THOMAS.

That was a whimsical noise. Zounds! that must be the players. Did you observe nothing else?

ROBIN.

Belike the quarrel first began between the gentry and a black-a-moor man.

Sir THOMAS.

With Friday! The public taste is debauch-
ed

ed; honest nature is too plain and simple for their vitiated palates! [*Enter* JULIET.] Juliet, Robin brings me the strangest account; some little disturbance; but I suppose it was soon settled again. Oh, but here comes Mr. Staytape, my taylor; he is a rational being; we shall be able to make something of him. [*Enter* STAYTAPE.] So, Staytape; what, is the third act over already?

STAYTAPE.
Over, Sir! no; nor never will be.

Sir THOMAS.
What do you mean?

STAYTAPE.
Cut short.

Sir THOMAS.
I don't comprehend you.

STAYTAPE.
Why, Sir, the poet has made a mistake in measuring the taste of the town; the goods, it seems, did not fit; so they return'd them upon the gentleman's hands.

Sir THOMAS.
Rot your affectation and quaintness, you puppy! speak plain.

STAYTAPE.
Why then, Sir, Robinson Crusoe is dead.

Sir THOMAS.
Dead!

STAYTAPE.
Ay; and, what is worse, will never rise any more. You will soon have all the particulars;

for there were four or five of your friends clofe at my heels.

Sir THOMAS.

Staytape, Juliet, run and ftop them; fay I am gone out; I am fick; I am engaged: but, whatever you do, be fure you don't let Bever come in. Secure of the victory, I invited them to the celebr---

STAYTAPE.

Sir, they are here.

Sir THOMAS.

Confound---

Enter PUFF, DACTYL, *and* RUST.

RUST.

Ay, truly, Mr. Puff, this is but a bitter beginning; then the young man muft turn himfelf to fome other trade.

PUFF.

Servant, Sir Thomas; I fuppofe you have heard the news of---

Sir THOMAS.

Yes, yes; I have been told it before.

DACTYL.

I confefs I did not fufpect it; but there is no knowing what effect thefe things will have, till they come on the ftage.

RUST.

For my part, I don't know much of thefe matters; but a couple of gentlemen near me, who feem'd fagacious enough too, declar'd that it was the vileft ftuff they ever had heard, and wonder'd the players would act it.

Yes;

DACTYL.

Yes; I don't remember to have seen a more general dislike.

PUFF.

I was thinking to ask you, Sir Thomas, for your interest with Mr. Bever about buying the copy:—but now no mortal would read it. Lord, Sir, it would not pay for paper and printing.

RUST.

I remember Kennet, in his Roman Antiquities, mentions a play of Terence's, Mr. Dactyl, that was terribly treated; but that he attributes to the people's fondness for certain funambuli, or rope-dancers; but I have not lately heard of any famous tumblers in town: Sir Thomas, have you?

Sir THOMAS.

How should I; do you suppose I trouble my head about tumblers?

RUST.

Nay, I did not---

BEVER, *speaking without.*

Not to be spoke with! Don't tell me, Sir; he must, he shall.

Sir THOMAS.

Mr. Bever's voice. If he is admitted in his present disposition, the whole secret will certainly out. Gentlemen, some affairs of a most interesting nature makes it impossible for me to have the honour of your company to-night; therefore I beg you would be so good as to---

RUST.

THE PATRON.

RUST.

Affairs! no bad news? I hope Miſs Julè is well.

Sir THOMAS.

Very well; but I am moſt exceedingly---

RUST.

I ſhall only juſt ſtay to ſee Mr. Bever. Poor lad! he will be moſt horribly down in the mouth: a little comfort won't come amiſs.

Sir THOMAS.

Mr. Bever, Sir! you won't ſee him here.

RUST.

Not here! why I thought I heard his voice but juſt now.

Sir THOMAS.

You are miſtaken Mr. Ruſt; but---

RUST.

May be ſo; then we will go. Sir Thomas, my compliments of condolance, if you pleaſe, to the poet.

Sir THOMAS.

Ay, ay.

DACTYL.

And mine; for I ſuppoſe we ſha'n't ſee him ſoon.

PUFF.

Poor gentleman! I warrant he won't ſhew his head for theſe ſix months.

RUST.

Ay, ay: indeed I am very ſorry for him; ſo tell him, Sir.

DACTYL and PUFF.

So are we.

RUST.

THE PATRON.

RUST.

Sir Thomas, your servant. Come, Gentlemen. By all this confusion in Sir Thomas, there must be something more in the wind than I know; but I will watch, I am resolv'd.

[*Exeunt.*

BEVER, *without.*

Rascals, stand by! I must, I will see him.

Enter BEVER.

So, Sir; this is delicate treatment, after all I have suffer'd.

Sir THOMAS.

Mr. Bever, I hope you don't---that is---

BEVER.

Well, Sir Thomas Lofty, what think you now of your Robinson Crusoe? a pretty performance!

Sir THOMAS.

Think, Mr. Bever! I think the public are blockheads; a tastelefs, stupid, ignorant tribe; and a man of genius deserves to be damn'd who writes any thing for them. But courage, dear Dick! the principals will give you what the people refuse; the closet will do you that justice the stage has deny'd: print your play.

BEVER.

My play! zounds, Sir, 'tis your own.

Sir THOMAS.

Speak lower, dear Dick; be moderate, my good, dear lad!

BEVER.

Oh, Sir Thomas, you may be easy enough;

you

you are fafe and fecure, remov'd far from that precipice that has dafhed me to pieces.

Sir THOMAS.

Dear Dick, don't believe it will hurt you. The critics, the real judges, will difcover in that piece fuch excellent talents---

BEVER.

No, Sir Thomas, no. I fhall neither flatter you nor myfelf; I have acquired a right to fpeak what I think. Your play, Sir, is a wretched performance; and in this opinion all mankind are united.

Sir THOMAS.

May be not.

BEVER.

If your piece had been greatly receiv'd, I would have declared Sir Thomas Lofty the author; if coldly, I would have owned it myfelf: but fuch difgraceful, fuch contemptible treatment! I own the burthen is too heavy for me; fo, Sir, you muft bear it yourfelf.

Sir THOMAS.

Me, dear Dick! what to become ridiculous in the decline of my life; to deftroy in one hour the fame that forty years has been building! that was the prop, the fupport of my age! Can you be cruel enough to defire it?

BEVER.

Zounds! Sir, and why muft I be your crutch? Would you have me become a voluntary victim; No, Sir, this caufe does not merit a martyrdom

Sir THOMAS.

I own myſelf greatly oblig'd; but perſevere, dear Dick, perſevere; you have time to recover your fame: I beg it with tears in my eyes. Another play will---

BEVER.

No, Sir Thomas; I have done with the ſtage: the Muſes and I meet no more.

Sir THOMAS.

Nay, there are various roads open in life.

BEVER.

Not one, where your piece won't purſue me. If I go to the bar, the ghoſt of this curs'd comedy will follow, and hunt me in Weſtminſter-hall: nay, when I die, it will ſtick to my memory, and I ſhall be handed down to poſterity with the author of Love in a Hollow Tree.

Sir THOMAS.

Then marry: you are a pretty ſmart figure; and your poetical talents---

BEVER.

And what fair would admit of my ſuit, or family wiſh to receive me? Make the caſe your own, Sir Thomas; would you?

Sir THOMAS.

With infinite pleaſure.

BEVER.

Then give me your niece; her hand ſhall ſeal up my lips.

Sir THOMAS.

What, Juliet? willingly. But are you ſerious, do you really admire the girl?

BEVER.

BEVER.

Beyond what words can exprefs. It was by her advice I confented to father your play.

Sir THOMAS.

What, is Juliet appriz'd? Here, Robin, John, run and call my niece hither this moment. That giddy baggage will blab all in an inftant.

BEVER.

You are miftaken; fhe is wifer than you are aware of.

Enter JULIET.

Sir THOMAS.

Oh, Juliet! you know what has happen'd.

JULIET.

I do, Sir.

Sir THOMAS.

Have you reveal'd this unfortunate fecret.

JULIET.

To no mortal, Sir Thomas.

Sir THOMAS.

Come, give me your hand. Mr. Bever, child, for my fake, has renounc'd the ftage, and the whole republic of letters; in return, I owe him your hand.

JULIET.

My hand! what to a poet hooted, hiffed, and exploded! You muft pardon me, Sir.

Sir THOMAS.

Juliet, a trifle: the moft they can fay of him is, that he is a little wanting in wit; and he has fo many brother writers to keep him in countenance, that now-a-days that is no reflection at all.

JULIET.

Then, Sir, your engagement to Mr. Ruſt.

Sir THOMAS.

I have found out the raſcal: he has been more impertinently ſevere on my play, than all the reſt put together; ſo that I am determined he ſhall be none of the man.

Enter RUST.

RUST.

Are you ſo, Sir? what, then I am to be ſacrific'd, in order to preſerve the ſecret that you are a blockhead. But you are out in your politics; before night it ſhall be known in all the coffee-houſes in town.

Sir THOMAS.

For Heaven's ſake, Mr. Ruſt!

RUST.

And to-morrow I will paragraph you in every news-paper; you ſhall no longer impoſe on the world; I will unmaſk you; the lion's ſkin ſhall hide you no longer.

Sir THOMAS.

Juliet! Mr. Bever! what can I do?

BEVER.

Sir Thomas, let me manage this matter. Harkee, old gentleman, a word in your ear: you remember what you have in your pocket?

RUST.

Hey! how! what?

BE-

BEVER.

The curiosity that has cost you so much pains.

RUST.

What, my Æneas! my precious relict of Troy!

BEVER.

You must give up that, or the lady.

JULIET.

How, Mr. Bever!

BEVER.

Never fear; I am sure of my man.

RUST.

Let me consider—As to the girl, girls are plenty enough; I can marry whenever I will: but my paper, my phenix, that springs fresh from the flames, that can never be match'd.--- Take her.

BEVER.

And, as you love your own secret, be careful of ours.

RUST.

I am dumb.

Sir THOMAS.

Now, Juliet.

JULIET.

You join me, Sir, to an unfortunate bard, but, to procure your peace---

Sir THOMAS.

You oblige me for ever. Now the secret dies with us four. My fault. I owe him much:

Be it your care to shew it;
And bless the man, tho' I have damn'd the poet.

FINIS.

www.ingramcontent.com/pod-product-compliance
Lightning Source LLC
Chambersburg PA
CBHW032046230426
43672CB00009B/1484